T0334326

Cambridge Elements ≡

Elements in Reinventing Capitalism
edited by
Arie Y. Lewin
Duke University
Till Talaulicar
University of Erfurt

THE FADING LIGHT OF DEMOCRATIC CAPITALISM

How Pervasive Cronyism and Restricted Suffrage Are Destroying Democratic Capitalism as a National Ideal ... And What To Do About It

Malcolm S. Salter
Harvard Business School

Shaftesbury Road, Cambridge CB2 8EA, United Kingdom

One Liberty Plaza, 20th Floor, New York, NY 10006, USA

477 Williamstown Road, Port Melbourne, VIC 3207, Australia

314–321, 3rd Floor, Plot 3, Splendor Forum, Jasola District Centre, New Delhi – 110025, India

103 Penang Road, #05–06/07, Visioncrest Commercial, Singapore 238467

Cambridge University Press is part of Cambridge University Press & Assessment, a department of the University of Cambridge.

We share the University's mission to contribute to society through the pursuit of education, learning and research at the highest international levels of excellence.

www.cambridge.org
Information on this title: www.cambridge.org/9781009587662

DOI: 10.1017/9781009587655

First published 2024

A catalogue record for this publication is available from the British Library

ISBN 978-1-009-58766-2 Hardback
ISBN 978-1-009-58764-8 Paperback
ISSN 2634-8950 (online)
ISSN 2634-8942 (print)

The Fading Light of Democratic Capitalism

How Pervasive Cronyism and Restricted Suffrage Are Destroying Democratic Capitalism as a National Ideal . . . And What To Do About It

Elements in Reinventing Capitalism

DOI: 10.1017/9781009587655
First published online: November 2024

Malcolm S. Salter
Harvard Business School

Author for correspondence: Malcolm S. Salter, msalter@hbs.edu

Abstract: This Element discusses how pervasive cronyism and restricted suffrage are destroying democratic capitalism as a national ideal and offers suggestions on how the promise of US-style democratic capitalism can be restored. Drawing on the principles of political equality, reciprocity, and power sharing advocated by political philosopher Danielle Allen, this Element suggest a series of practical steps to make our economic and political markets more democratic by curbing cronyism and expanding citizens' access to the political processes governing our nation. It also discusses how private corporations can become more "democracy supporting." It ends with some reflections on the moral culture required to restore and sustain public faith in democratic capitalism as a system of economic and political governance.

Keywords: democratic capitalism, cronyism, universal suffrage, political equality, power sharing

ISBNs: 9781009587662 (HB), 9781009587648 (PB), 9781009587655 (OC)
ISSNs: 2634-8950 (online), 2634-8942 (print)

Contents

1 Introduction

After World War II, the social construct we call "democratic capitalism" became for many North Americans and Western Europeans a celebrated ideal. In the half century following World War II, democratic capitalism brought Americans a period of singular economic growth and prosperity – marked, in part, by the highest level of average annual income in the world.[1] Universal high school education and the G. I. Bill (the Servicemen's Readjustment Act of 1944), which sent many veterans to university, supported this economic record, making the United States one of the most educated nations in the world and enabling unprecedented rates of technological innovation and economic expansion. Under an antitrust regime that ensured fair competition in an open economy and protected consumers from predatory business practices, productive competition among established firms was preserved, while new business formation reached unprecedented levels. Job growth coupled with an increasingly higher standard of living followed. At the same time, Americans' access to the nation's political process also expanded as the right to vote broadened and received new protections with the passage of the Voting Rights Act of 1965.

Although this era of exceptional growth and prosperity was interrupted in the 1970s by deep recession and high inflation, an economic boom during the 1990s brought a period of steady job creation, lower inflation, rising productivity, and a surging stock market. This recovery was accompanied by a growing belief among many Americans that laissez-faire capitalism (and the deregulation of industries such as banking and airlines) was the best way back to prosperity. The arc of this fifty-year economic history was sufficient to convince many Americans that, despite its intermittent breakdowns and corruptions, capitalism was an acceptable economic system – even one to be celebrated, as long as a well-developed political democracy could rein in the excesses of free markets and hold private parties controlling the factors of production accountable to the public will. Gradually, the broad appeal of our unique, if imperfect, pairing of capitalism and democracy blended into the imagery of what many Americans believe our nation stands for. For some citizens, like me, who matured during

---

[1] From 1945 to 1981, US gross domestic product (GDP) increased from $228 billion to just under $1.7 trillion. In 1981, after decades of economic growth by other industrialized nations, US industry still maintained a third of the world's total output – compared with 16 percent for Germany and 14 percent for Britain, according to Alfred D. Chandler Jr, *Scope and Scale: The Dynamics of Industrial Capitalism*, Harvard University Press, 1990, p. 47. The benefits this economic growth and resulting industrial scale, coupled with the success of organized labor in bargaining for wage and benefit increases, persisted well into the twenty-first century: In 2018, US average annual income was (GNP divided by population) was more than $56,000, compared with $9,850 for Russia and $8,250 for China, according to data assembled by the OECD, World Bank, and International Monetary Fund.

those prosperous postwar years, democratic capitalism has long been considered a cornerstone of our national ideology and identity, expressing our collective hopes and ideals.

More recently, however, survey after survey has shown that its two vital building blocks – democracy and capitalism – have suffered dramatic setbacks in popular trust and confidence,[2] which raises three questions about its status and prospects as our espoused ideology. What, precisely, does "democratic capitalism" mean in the US context? Can this understanding of democratic capitalism continue to serve as a realistic aspiration for the United States in the future? If the answer is no, how can this idea be restored as an illuminating ideal?

In addressing these questions, I begin by defining in Section 2 what democratic capitalism includes as a system of economic and political governance and how inherent frictions between democracy and capitalism have, until recently, been either accommodated or tolerated in the US setting.

Next, in Section 3, I explain how the toxic combination of pervasive cronyism and restricted suffrage limits the political voice and influence of ordinary citizens and puts the fragile relationship between capitalism and democracy at risk. Here, I discuss how – in the context of historically high levels of income and wealth inequality – this "toxic duo" poses a deep-seated threat to popular support for democratic capitalism as a national ideal. It does so by inflaming popular feelings that our system of economic and political governance is not only rigged in favor of wealthy and powerful elites but is also unaccountable to a large swath of the voting public. In other words, this toxic duo has created a governance system that is neither truly democratic nor truly capitalist.

Cronyism in this context refers to special interests influencing and bending the political system to private advantage. It typically involves the capture of

---

[2] Several surveys have documented rising public anxiety and criticism of American-style democracy as not serving the public's needs. In 2017, Common Cause reported surveys showing that 71 percent of Americans agreed that our system of democracy had reached "a dangerous low point." The comparable statistic for the 1960s was about 30 percent. More recently, in the run-up to the 2022 midterm elections, the Pew Research Center reported that about six in ten Americans were dissatisfied with the way democracy is working in the country. During the 2022 elections, the future of democracy was the second-most important voting issue after the economy for 60 percent of Democrats and 66 percent of Republicans. With respect to capitalism, the 2020 Edelman Trust Barometer reported that 47 percent of those Americans surveyed agreed that "capitalism as it exists today does more harm than good." (By comparison, Edelman found that 69 percent of people in France had lost faith in capitalism; 55 percent in Germany; and 53 percent in the UK.) Fewer than half of the eighteen-to-twenty-nine-year-olds in the United States now support capitalism, according to a 2018 Gallop survey. Finally, a recent *Wall Street Journal*/ NORC survey found that only 36 percent of voters said the American dream holds true, down from 48 percent in 2016 and 53 percent in 2012. For a full report, see Aaron Zitner, "Voters See American Dream Slipping Out of Reach," *The Wall Street Journal*, Available at https://www.wsj .com/us-news/american-dream-out-of-reach-poll-3b774892 November 24, 2023.

legislative and regulatory rulemaking by small but powerful groups of elites operating largely in the private sector. Cronyism greatly diminishes the democratic aspect of democratic capitalism.

Restricted suffrage presents a comparable threat to democratic capitalism. It refers to matters such as citizens' restricted rights to vote, restricted rights to gain ballot access and run for office, and, more generally, difficulties participating in political processes and accessing the instruments of government that enable citizens to exercise their right to shape civil society.

The combined effects of citizens living under a governance system that is increasingly perceived to be dominated by special interests and not subject to control by the voting public is, inevitably, marked by increased political indifference and the capture of disconnected and disenchanted voters by political madcaps and demagogues.

In response to this unsettling political scenario, I turn in Section 4 to the steps needed to restore democratic capitalism as an illuminating ideal and realistic aspiration for the United States. The critical first step is weakening the fatal grip of cronyism and the restricted voice on our political economy. I discuss why such a restoration will require adjusting the imbalance of power between (1) wealthy and influential parties – both in business and politics – who manipulate society's rules accordingly to their private interests and (2) ordinary citizens who possess minimal countervailing power and value different political and economic outcomes than those of their wealthier and more powerful compatriots. I anchor this discussion in the bedrock principle of a just political economy – *political equality* – and two facets of political equality, namely, *reciprocity* and *power sharing*. This discussion, I hasten to add, is *not* an argument for limiting wealth creation and the accumulation potential of capitalism, but is instead an argument for a more democratic pathway to achieving the economic and social benefits that it offers.

Until this point in my discussion, I focus primarily on the corroding dynamics of our economic and political markets. In Section 5, I expand the scope of analysis. Here, I discuss how the ideal of democratic capitalism is diminished by firms' traditional hierarchical decision structure (our primary social institution) modeled on centuries of military chains of command and control, where little attention is paid to employee participation in decisions affecting their personal well-being. I then identify ways in which these essentially nondemocratic regimes can become more "democracy-supporting."[3]

---

[3] This is Danielle Allen's phrase. See *Justice by Means of Democracy*, The University of Chicago Press, 2023, pp. 170–176.

I conclude with Section 6, which addresses the norms and values required to support the work of democracy reformers in both the private and public sectors. Today, democratic capitalism suffers from a moral culture that celebrates self-interest; tolerates cronyism and outsized political influence by small groups of wealthy individuals and corporations; and condones restrictions on the voice and influence of ordinary citizens, whose democratic role is to express the public interest and hold elected representatives accountable to their campaign promises and other public responsibilities. What's required to support the idea of democratic capitalism – as a cornerstone of our national ideology – is a broadly based effort to nudge social norms and values away from maximizing personal utility and the exclusive pursuit of private interest toward a more relational culture based on the moral principles of political equality and reciprocity, and the artful practice of power sharing. Socializing these principles and norms must include wider reporting of, and publicity for, the reciprocal exchanges and mutual gains that have already been created, and are being created today, in innovative power-sharing forums and other relational environments around the country. Continued field-based research on contemporary experiments in democracy-supporting governance, in both business and politics, is required to support the efforts of current and would-be evangelists to restore democratic capitalism. I provide several examples of past shifts in moral values in the United States based on research, publication, and publicity of that research, as well as the evangelical work of reformers who built a strong powerbase to influence a shift in the values and norms within the business community, electoral politics, and the judiciary.

In the appendix, titled "The Problematic Doctrine of Shareholder Wealth Maximization," I describe how the canonization of the shareholder wealth maximization doctrine as the only legitimate expression of corporate purpose over the past forty years has provided a strong rationale and great financial incentive for corporations to disengage as a moral force in our political economy by focusing executives' attention on pursuing institutional and personal wealth maximization (self-interest) – to the extent of compromising the fairness and justness of our system of economic and political governance and serving as a barrier to the restoration of true democratic capitalism. I also comment on the doctrine's conceptual flaws as a normative economic concept.

2 The Idea of Democratic Capitalism

2.1 Democratic Capitalism Defined

Democratic capitalism refers to a man-made system of relationships and rules governing the behavior of economic actors. As a social construct, it is a system of economic and political governance in which the conduct of market economies is shaped by rules and regulations worked out by democratically elected representatives and public officials whose primary responsibility is to serve the will of the people.[4] These rules and regulations determine the way in which markets and firms are structured, sustained, regulated, and held accountable. When played out in a civil society capable of compromise and peaceful negotiations (and where political power is diffused among the public rather than concentrated in the hands of a few), such a governance system ideally provides a means to align competing economic and noneconomic priorities and distribute the benefits of economic activity according to society's collective will.

Commonly assumed goals of democratic capitalism (i.e., reflecting society's collective will) include economic prosperity that enables an increasing standard of living for all citizens, good jobs for those who can work, security for those who need it, eliminating special privileges for the few, and, as an overarching goal, institutional support for human justice.[5] In my view, and that of many fellow citizens, there's much work to be done to achieve these goals.

Democratic capitalism relies on two, interrelated sub-governance regimes. The first pertains to *economic governance* (capitalism) and ideally encompasses the ways in which relatively free and open markets (1) enable the supply and demand for goods and services to be matched by self-interested consumers seeking to maximize their preferences; (2) coordinate the decisions of savers and investors through the price mechanism; and, in the end, (3) allocate resources to their most productive end use. In addition to its allocative function, capitalism also serves a creative function by providing strong incentives for innovation and making the benefits of innovation widely available to the public at large. Capitalism also provides incentives for millions of problem-solving experiments to occur every day, for competition to select the best solutions, and for scaling-up and making the best solutions available.[6] At the level of *ideal theory*, the capitalist form of economic governance presumes a minimalist role for government, freedom from coercion, and freedom to buy and sell anything that one has created or owns. Whenever government is permitted or invited to intervene, its role should be limited to replicating a well-functioning market's outcomes.

---

[4] The idea of capitalism as a system of governance is developed in great detail by Bruce R. Scott in *Capitalism: Its Origins and Evolution as a System of Governance*, Springer, 2011.

[5] As initially articulated by President Franklin Roosevelt in January 1941 and restated by Martin Wolf in *The Crisis of Democratic Capitalism*, Penguin Press, 2023, pp. 229–231.

[6] Nick Hanauer and Eric Beinhocker have effectively argued this point in "Capitalism Redefined," *Democracy: A Journal of Ideas*, no. 31, Winter 2014 and Colin Mayer, *Prosperity*, Oxford University Press, 2018.

In practice, significant departures exist from this capitalist model of economic governance – such as legislation setting minimum working hours or wages, protections against discrimination, state ownership of selected firms and industries, and targeted industry subsidies, and much more. Relatedly, there is great variety in the pattern of economic governance across nations. As many students of capitalism have pointed out, France's system of economic governance is not identical to that of the United States; Sweden is not Italy; the UK is not South Korea; and Japan is not Singapore.[7] Each of these nations differs according to social and political preferences related to individual freedoms, the degree of private ownership of capital, public authorities' regulatory intervention, the existence and nature of their social security systems, the incentives available for risk-taking and entrepreneurship, the tolerance level of economic inequality, taxation, and much more.

Across all variants of capitalism, however, a common feature is the role of markets (rather than centralized government planning) in allocating capital. Yet, despite this shared feature of capitalist economies, the presence of market activity does not by itself define the essence of capitalism. Instead, the central feature of all capitalist systems are private property rights, sanctioned by political authority, that enable reasonably efficient market exchanges. These property rights give private economic actors the right to own, trade, and control property according to their interests, to invest capital as they see fit, and to reap the bulk of subsequent returns.[8]

In the United States, the principle of private property rights has been deeply embedded as a national ideal since the founding of our nation as a commercial republic. Our Constitution's framers were familiar with John Locke and Adam Smith, whose work argued that every man had a property right to whatever he acquired or created through his own labor, and that property rights were indispensable to the success of the new nation. James Madison, Thomas Jefferson, John Adams, and Alexander Hamilton, among others, found common ground in the idea that the right to property was both a guarantee of people's legal rights and essential to liberty. Thus, the notion that a market-based system of reciprocal exchanges of property in what we now call the private sector contributes to society's well-being has been part of the American DNA and the American dream since the founding of our nation. As many scholars have

---

[7] See Michael Novak, "Democratic Capitalism," *National Review*, September 24, 2013, and *The Spirit of Democratic Capitalism*, Simon & Schuster, 1982; Chandler, *Scale and Scope*; Thomas K. McCraw, *Creating Modern Capitalism*, Harvard University Press, 1998; and Scott, *Capitalism*.

[8] David Upham, "The Primacy of Property Rights and the American Founding," *Foundation of Economic Education*, February 1, 1998.

documented, it took less than a century after the Constitution ratified the importance of private property for large, hierarchical firms (in mining, manufacturing, transportation, and trade) to arise from their modest beginnings to populate an ever-expanding capitalist economy.

The democracy component of democratic capitalism took a good deal longer to take hold than the capitalism component. It did not become an important modifier of capitalism until slavery was abolished in the nineteenth century and universal suffrage was instituted in the twentieth century. With political and economic reforms legislated during the 1930s and then after World War II during the 1950s and 1960s, the idea of truly democratic capitalism began to take on strong sponsorship and broad credibility in contrast to previously competing ideologies such as democratic socialism and communism. Such ideologies had attracted some citizens during the Great Depression before World War II, which takes us to the second governance regime comprising democratic capitalism.

The second governance regime relates, of course, to political governance (as in a representative democracy). It encompasses a mix of political processes, laws, and regulations that set the rules of the game for decentralized decision-making throughout the economy. In a functioning democracy, it is the people who hold the ultimate power to determine whether these rules and procedures – and the exercise of political power and governance flowing from them – are democratic or need to be changed. A necessary condition for democratic oversight is people's full participation rights in the political process, starting with the right to vote and hold political office. A functioning democracy thus rests on the bedrock principles of popular sovereignty and political equality.[9]

Another notable feature of representative democracy is "majority rule" as a mechanism for aggregating public preferences and translating them into policy that reflects society's collective will. This mechanism can work as long as majority rule does not trample the interests and political rights of minority parties – a possibility identified as "the tyranny of the majority" by Alexis de Tocqueville 200 years ago. In practice, limits are typically placed on majority rule in representative democracies by unelected and nominally independent institutions such as courts or central banks.[10] In addition, any democracy worth

---

[9] Political equality includes five defining characteristics according to Danielle Allen (*Justice by Means of Democracy*, pp. 36–37): freedom from domination; equal access to the instruments of government; good knowledge processes; reciprocity or mutual responsiveness; and co-ownership of political institutions such as congresses and judicial offices at the federal, state, and local levels, which effectively puts a limit on the (inappropriate) use of these institutions.

[10] For a discussion of the philosophical and practical limitations of majority rule, see George Will, "The Limits of Majority Rule," *National Affairs*, Summer 2001, www.nationalaffairs.com/publications/detail/the-limits-of-majority-rule.

its name requires that winners in the competition for power between political parties accept the legitimacy of defeat. Accepting the legitimacy of elections and the results of other competitions for political power requires acts of sacrifice for democracy to confer stability and legitimacy. As Danielle Allen explains, because most transactions in business and politics cannot be a perfect bargain for all parties, voluntary sacrifice is required to build and maintain trust by drawing people into a "network of mutual obligation" where those who benefit from a sacrifice see themselves "as recipients of a gift that they must honor and (someday) reciprocate."[11]

Not that networks of mutual obligation are easy to form or maintain. If we think of democracy as being a form of competition in political markets between self-interested politicians whose primary goal is to reap the rewards of holding office for the votes of citizens whose primary goal is to extract the greatest benefits possible from the parties in office, as argued by economists Joseph Schumpeter and Anthony Downs, then the opportunities for a wide range of self-serving, anti-competitive, and community-fractioning behaviors become readily apparent.[12] In such a transactional political marketplace, where "political parties behave like firms, politicians like entrepreneurial managers and voters like customers," there are many incentives for both citizens and office holders to employ any activity not otherwise prohibited by law to further their special interests and ignore the shared interests of a more inclusive polis.[13] Such activities are the subject of Section 3.

As important as it is to understand what the system of economic and political governance of democratic capitalism entails, it is equally important to understand that the relationship between the two governance regimes is changing constantly in response to shifting conceptions of corporate purpose and political context. In the United States, for example, we know these evolving relationships left notable historical footprints. The late nineteenth and early twentieth centuries, a period now characterized as Managerial Capitalism, saw newly emergent large corporations seeking ways to coexist with an evolving democratic system that had formerly been based on patronage in seeking votes and staffing federal departments. To protect their privileged status in American life and create a stable and predictable regulatory structure, business leaders began to push the political system and federal bureaucracy to eliminate

---

[11] Danielle Allen, *Talking to Strangers: Anxieties of Citizenship since Brown v. Board of Education*, University of Chicago Press, 2004, p. 111.

[12] Joseph A. Schrumpeter, *Capitalism, Socialism, and Democracy*, Harper & Row, 1942 and Anthony Downs, *An Economic Theory of Democracy*, Harper, 1957.

[13] Jacob Jensen, "Anthony Downs and the Equilibrium Theory of Democracy." https://doi.org/10.4000/oeconomia.10467.

patronage-based governance. By the mid-1950s after the Great Depression, the New Deal, and two world wars, a new era now referred to as Stakeholder Capitalism began to take shape. During this period, which followed intensive debates about the role of business in society during the 1930s, executives of large corporations found it useful to begin speaking of enlightened self-interest in their corporate governance and start working with political authorities and organized labor to expand infrastructure, education, housing, and taxes and to enforce the rule of law and public accountability. Stakeholder capitalism was not a complete takeover of American capitalism, but it was an important influence in those days, and its influence persists with other interpretations of democratic capitalism. After the economic shocks of the 1970s, another form of capitalism known as Shareholder Capitalism captured the imagination and policies of the business community as a practical, financial overlay of the more general postwar ideal of democratic capitalism. Milton Friedman, a Nobel Prize winner in economics from the University of Chicago, became a leading spokesperson for shareholder capitalism in the early 1970s by arguing that corporations have no moral obligation other than increasing profits for shareholders (within constrains of the law and accepted social norms).[14] Any responsibility to society or the body politic beyond profit-making was decidedly off the table. Over the past fifty years, during which economists, business executives, and reformers of all stripes have forcefully debated the role of the corporation in modern society, a greater recognition that corporations cannot ignore issues important to the public has again emerged in the business community. This holds even as public corporations, large private equity firms, and institutional investors such as state pension funds stand by their unwavering commitment to shareholder wealth maximization as a top priority.

The history of continued mutation and evolution of capitalism and its relationship with an evolving democratic polity is vastly more technical and political than indicated here. But this capsule history shows that, as a social construct, one would expect national forms of capitalism to evolve over time as the body politic and its political vision changes. No steady state exists in capitalism or democratic capitalism. It also suggests that we are inevitably witnessing changes – for better or worse – in the development path and prospects of democratic capitalism as a mutually reinforcing system of economic and political governance.[15]

---

[14] Milton Friedman, "The Social Responsibility of Business Is to Increase Profits," *New York Times Magazine*, September 13, 1970.

[15] Scott stressed this point in his detailed study of the origins and evolution of capitalism. Scott, *Capitalism*, 2011.

2.2 Managed Contradictions between Capitalism and Democracy

There are good reasons to expect the two governance regimes that we think of as capitalism and democracy to be mutually reinforcing and thus resilient to external challenges posed by less democratic regimes and self-inflicted wounds (in the form of policy errors and corruption). For example, American economist Rebecca Henderson points out that democratic government protects and strengthens free markets by providing important protections such as (1) an impartial justice system, (2) a marketplace where prices can reflect true costs rather than other arbitrary charges, (3) real competition leading to persistent innovation, and (4) freedom of opportunity through the provision of education and access to health care and other necessary public services.[16]

In addition, social philosopher Michael Novak has long argued that in the long run, democracy is a necessary condition for the success of capitalism because (1) more autocratic forms of capitalism ignore the interests of non-corporate constituencies vital to sustained economic success and (2) democratic institutions are critical in securing the perceived legitimacy of capitalism and, with this, social stability.[17] In other words, capitalism needs democracy to work as a moral engine of prosperity, and democracy needs capitalism to support the social contract (or "the deal") between the state and the people. Novak also argues that the survivability of democratic capitalism depends on the moral culture or "moral ecology" surrounding it – comprised of virtues such as creativity, self-sacrifice, self-restraint, and disciplined work. Whereas Novak's model of democratic capitalism is exceedingly difficult to live up to, cultivating the right moral ecology is both the next generation's major challenge and major reward. The history of democratic capitalism's successes and self-inflicted failures over the past forty years shows how on target Novak's assessment is.

Danish political scientist Torben Iversen and British political scientist and economist David Soskice similarly argue that in advanced economies, democracy and capitalism tend to strengthen one another, as well as the survivability of democratic capitalism, provided three stabilizing pillars are in place: (1) a strong government, which constrains the power of large firms and labor unions and ensures competitive markets; (2) a sizeable middle class forming a political bloc that insists on sharing in the prosperity created by a capitalist society; and (3) large firms, even in the era of globalization, that remain sufficiently rooted in their original habitat to be taxed so the government can spend on middle class

---

[16] Rebecca Henderson, "The Business Case for Saving Democracy," *Harvard Business Review*, March 10, 2020.

[17] Novak, "Democratic Capitalism."

priorities.[18] (Widespread profit shifting by large corporations into tax havens around the world with very low tax rates certainly weakens this pillar.)

Finally, Martin Wolf, the long-time chief economic commenter at the *Financial Times*, characterizes the symbiotic relationships between market capitalism and liberal democracy as "complementary opposites." The two are complementary in the sense that they share the idea of the right of people to make their own choices and to shape their own lives – whether by freely voicing opinion and exercising the right to vote in political markets or freely buying and selling property in economic markets. This commonality is part of the emotional and ideological glue supporting the vision of democratic capitalism. Another concept, according to Wolf, is the understanding that capitalism supplies democracy with economic resources, whereas democracy supplies capitalism with legitimacy. But Wolf also sees dissonance between capitalism and democracy. While capitalism seeks private financial returns, a democratic electorate focuses on different community outcomes: economic security; insurance against unemployment, ill health, and old age; laws that protect the public from exploitation; tax paying by the wealthy; and so on. This fragile symbiosis between capitalism and democracy – which Wolf calls "the great story of democratic capitalism" – can only be maintained by compromise and cooperation among the social, economic, and political actors in the governance system that we refer to as democratic capitalism. Wolf sees this cooperative marriage at risk, but salvable.[19]

Standing apart from these cautious optimists is Wolfgang Streeck, a German economic sociologist, and prolific student of capitalism, who takes a more apocalyptic position than any of the philosophers and social scientists mentioned above.[20] Streeck argues that we are now witnessing the end of capitalism caused by a variety of disorders including, among other things, (1) a decline in economic growth, which leaves fewer resources with which democratically elected governments can settle distributional conflict; (2) "oligarchic redistribution" leading to ever-increasing income and wealth inequality; (3) corporate fraud and moral decay, such as Enron, WorldCom, and banks' price-fixing of interest rates; and (4) global disarray caused largely by the declining performance of the US economy, a series of destructive financial crises, rising levels of sovereign debt with attendant risks of default and bailouts of national and international banks, and increasing lack of

---

[18] Torben Iversen and David Soskice, *Democracy and Prosperity*, Princeton University Press, 2019.

[19] Wolf, *The Crisis of Democratic Capitalism*, especially Chapters 2 and 9.

[20] Wolfgang Streek, "The Crises of Democratic Capitalism," *New Left Review*, September/October 2011, and "How Will Capitalism End?" *New Left Review*, May/June 2014.

confidence in the US dollar as a reserve currency. Streeck's ominous analysis includes a useful reminder that dissonance does indeed exist between capitalism and democracy, as Wolf and others are aware. This dissonance, Streeck argues, is rooted in conflicting principles of resource allocation held by each governance regime – one based on the free play of market forces, the other based on social need or entitlement, as expressed and certified by the collective choices of democratic politics. Under democratic capitalism, both principles need to be honored simultaneously, which, logically speaking, can only be achieved under two simultaneous conditions: (1) when the system of economic and political governance can deliver sufficient economic returns to both capitalists and the demos to keep the delicate balance (trade-offs) between free enterprise and political democracy in place, and (2) in the presence of widely shared virtues such as self-restraint, honesty, trustworthiness, truthfulness, and respect for the law. For Streeck, this is a tall order of conditions to be met.

Were he alive today, German philosopher, economist, sociologist, historian, and political theorist Karl Marx would disagree philosophically with the idea that democratic capitalism could survive under either Wolf's or Streeck's conditions. Marx argued in *The Communist Manifesto* back in 1848 that democracy will always be sacrificed to protect capitalism, and that capitalism, in turn, makes democracy impossible. Under capitalism, the state is most concerned with political democracy, not economic democracy. And, in any case, even in the most liberal states, governments have little or no formal power over private capital. For all these reasons, if we want true democracy, Marx tells us to forget capitalism. A contemporary historian studying the rise of "neoliberal globalization" following World War II adds a historical dimension to Marx's claim.

Quinn Slobodian, a Canadian historian, writes in his history of the rise of global neoliberalism that neoliberals such as E. A. Hayek and his academic followers – who believed in global laissez-faire government (including self-regulating markets, shrunken states, and the reduction of all human motivation to the rational self-interest of Homo economicus) – did not see democracy and capitalism as either synonymous or mutually reinforcing. Instead, democracy is viewed by neoliberals as a problem for capitalism.[21] According to Slobodian, what democracy means for the early neoliberals is "successive waves of clamoring, demanding masses, always threatening to push the functioning market economy off its tracks."[22] Democracy is also perceived as a danger to capitalism by legitimizing the redistribution of capitalism's gains. For these

---

[21] Quinn Slobodian, *Globalists*, Harvard University Press, 2018.   [22] Ibid., p. 17.

reasons, a central goal of the neoliberal project is to build global "safeguards against the disruptive capacity of democracy."[23]

One does not need to be either a Marxist or a neoliberal to imagine other points of contradiction between the two governance regimes. Consider, for example, the critical matter of who holds "decision rights" in our political economy. In a true democracy based on political equality among citizens, people make laws and public policies as equal citizens, principally through free and fair elections. Seen in this light, democracy is an *inclusive governance regime* based on the belief that every citizen should have an equal say in decisions affecting their lives. Under capitalism, however, private property has evolved into industrial and commercial hierarchies where legally protected property rights confer dominant decision power to business owners, investors, and their agents over the deployment of capital and the governance of privately owned firms (where 85 percent of the US workforce is employed). In marked contrast to other players in the economy, the decision rights and power of capitalists in the private sector often dominate the decision rights of all others, and the result is an *exclusive governance regime* with restricted decision-making rights both within and beyond firm boundaries (which happen to be our nation's dominant social institution). With economic control and decision-making largely relegated to privately owned corporations, whose executives live with unrelenting demands of shareholders seeking above-average returns on their investments, democracy's core principles of popular sovereignty and political equality take a big hit.

The extent of capital's dominance in the conduct of today's business operations is best seen in the remarkable canonization of shareholder wealth maximization over the past forty years as the only legitimate expression of business purpose. The adoption of this doctrine by the business community represents a major shift in corporate values away from those that prevailed in the 1930s under a more stakeholder-oriented version of capitalism. More specifically, this doctrine offers incentives for corporate executives and powerful insiders to place their self-interests way ahead of the interests and concerns of other constituencies of the enterprise. For example, corporations can create stock-based compensation plans for executives that guarantee huge rewards for increasing their companies' stock price, even though increases in stock price may have little to do with creating long-term economic value of the enterprise. Furthermore, following from this executive compensation regime, corporations provide incentives for executives to invest in short-term gains through stock buybacks (which has the effect of increasing the earnings per share, stock price,

---

[23] Ibid., p. 272.

and wealth position for executives holding stock options and stock grants) rather than investing corporate capital in risky long-term business development.

With very high personal and shareholder gains on the line, the natural tendency of rational, self-interested corporate management is to preserve and structure the economic game in ways that best serve their interests by "investing" in electoral politics and legislative/regulatory lobbying. In addition, the idea of shareholder wealth maximization provides a seemingly rational justification for executives to lock themselves into a perpetually dominant bargaining position over the distribution of corporate benefits vis-à-vis other participants in the enterprise – such as employees and local communities – who have a legitimate claim, under law and custom, on the firm's resources. (See Appendix for a detailed explanation of this economic doctrine and the challenges it presents for the future of democratic capitalism.)

Serious consequences exist for this corporate governance regime – namely, those pertaining to the distribution of economic benefits created under market capitalism. There are several stories here. The more encouraging story recounts the widely distributed economic benefits of American-style capitalism that flow from its unprecedented rates of innovation, despite its flaws. This includes many quality-of-life improvements (in refrigeration, communication, transportation, and health care, for example) and sustained GDP and job growth.

On the GDP growth front, the *Economist* recently pointed out that America today accounts for 58 percent of the G7's GDP, up from 40 percent in 1990.[24] Similarly, as noted in the Introduction, American income per capita has been higher and steadily increasing since 1990 over that of Western Europeans, and investment returns in the S&P 500 Index of American companies (supporting our vital pension funds, as just one example) has outperformed the returns of a similar index of non-American, rich-world stocks by a factor of four. Yet, there is also a less-encouraging, politically troubling story that recounts: how the real (purchasing power adjusted) wages of many US workers have barely budged over the past forty years; how job growth has been capped by the shift of low-value added production to lower labor cost nations, leaving many small towns and communities hollowed out; how income and wealth inequality is higher in the United States than in almost any other developed country, suggesting that only a small segment of society appears to be gaining from GDP growth; how the financial security of many citizens has declined; and how the rate of intergenerational economic mobility is below that of other advanced

---

[24] "America's Economic Performance Is a Marvel to Behold," *The Economist,* April 13, 2023. www.bloomberg.com/news/articles/2023-03-28/anti-esg-crusades-in-gop-states-stumble-amid-pension-pushback?embedded-checkout=true.

economies. These latter trends are emblematic of ongoing frictions between capitalism and democracy.

Fortunately, one of the important features of America's democratic-capitalist political economy is that some of the most essential contradictions have been contained by the body politic in recent decades. Past containment strategies include a combination of market and financial regulations (beyond the abolition of slavery) aimed at minimizing the ills of capitalism associated with unbridled personal gain, monopoly and restraint of trade, securities manipulation, and environmental degradation; the introduction of maximum working hours and minimum wage legislation; anti-discrimination measures; increasingly redistributive tax policy; and the introduction and expansion of publicly funded mechanisms to provide safety nets for people injured by economic change and dislocation. In addition, the voice of the trade union movement, although only embracing a small minority of the work force (10 percent today, down from 20 percent in the early 1980s), has been effective in balancing the dominance of capital's decision right in some industries and protecting and promoting workers' interests in the political marketplace. Relatedly, on the wage front, the government's pursuit of an accommodating monetary policy allowed collective bargaining for higher wages and full employment to coexist at the expense of an accelerating rate of inflation. This arrangement was critical to maintaining a stable democracy during the turbulent 1980s and 1990s (although it was not a sustainable strategy over the long run). Finally, an increasing number of influential entrepreneurs and business leaders have understood, stood for, and governed their enterprises according to the idea that successful businesses need to view themselves as cooperative systems, not simply vehicles to maximize shareholders' wealth. In marked contrast to emphasizing maximizing shareholders' value or wealth, their espoused purposes reflect a different moral culture best summarized as creating shared value for all the firm's constituencies or, more simply, "making a decent profit in a decent way." Rebecca Henderson provides several instructive examples in her recent book on reimagining capitalism.[25]

While these accommodations and economic benefits may have preserved the promise of democratic capitalism as a credible governance model in the past, it is questionable that they are sufficient to preserve democratic capitalism as stable or practical governance model for America in the future. Unless a renovated democratic capitalism can successfully reverse the decline of public trust in both large corporations and in capitalism as a system of economic governance, the days of democratic capitalism serving as an illuminating

---

[25] Rebecca Henderson, *Reimaging Capitalism in a World on Fire*, Public Affairs, 2020.

ideal and realistic national aspiration will end. This is what repeated polling is telling us. Over the past decade, and in the aftermath of the 2008 financial crisis and the great recession, surveys by Gallop, Frank Lutz, Harvard's Institute of Politics, and the Edelman Trust Barometer have all shown that only about one in five respondents trust US big business, and that throughout the industrialized world only 20 percent feel that the current system of political economy is working for them. It is highly unlikely that these opinions will change without substantial reform in our system of economic and political governance.

As observed by leading free market economists Raghuram Rajan and Luigi Zingales, "democratic capitalism's greatest problem is not that it will destroy itself economically, as Marx, would have it, but that it may lose its political support."[26]

3 The Fading Light of Democratic Capitalism

To reverse declining public trust in today's democratic capitalism and preserve the idea of democratic capitalism as a practical ideal for the United States going forward, we need to attack two cancers that are assaulting our system of economic and political governance: cronyism and restrictions on the voice and political influence of ordinary citizens.

There are, of course, additional malignancies residing in our body politic that adversely affect public trust in our current political economy, including years of unequal sharing of gains in income growth and historically high levels of income and wealth inequality. When the top 1 percent of income earners capture 50 percent of the overall economic growth of real incomes per family over 1993–2018, that hardly leads to the feeling that the system is working for most citizens, even if their family income is growing.[27] And when wealth becomes concentrated in the hands of high-income earners, as in the United States where 70 percent of the total wealth is owned by the top 10 percent of earners, that only compounds the dissatisfaction of the remaining 90 percent with their disadvantaged status and a system in which they feel trapped.[28] This concentration of wealth also enables powerful and self-serving influence by the few over politics through funding political parties and candidates, as well as lobbying Congress and regulatory agencies.

---

[26] Raghuram Rajan and Luigi Zingales, *Saving Capitalism from the Capitalists*, Princeton University Press, 2004.

[27] Emmanuel Saez, "Striking It Richer: The Evolution of Top Incomes in the United States" (Updated with 2018 estimates), February 2020, http://elsa.berkeley.edu/~saez/TabFig2018prel.xls.

[28] Statistica, "Wealth Distribution in the United States in the Second Quarter of 2023," http://elsa.berkeley.edu/~saez/TabFig2018prel.xls.

These and other outcomes have given many Americans reason to believe that society has stopped working for them. Such outcomes are not easily reversed in a world where economic rulemaking and policy preferences remain under the increasing influence of a small, powerful, and politically unaccountable elite comprised of wealthy individuals and corporations. Here is where the twin cancers of cronyism and restricted political voice pose special risks to democratic capitalism. Together they inhibit, rather than enable, people to improve their material and political well-being, which are fundamental promises of democratic capitalism.

3.1 Capitalism's Malady: Pervasive Cronyism

Cronyism, also known as crony capitalism, refers to a world where economic success (or survival) depends on developing close relationships between businesspeople and government officials rather than independently achieved success in a competitive market.

Put somewhat differently, crony capitalism is a form of corruption wherein private parties make undue profit from abuse of public authority. It is corrupt because it undermines integrity in the discharge of duty by public officials.[29]

In its most basic form, it is useful to think of cronyism as a two-sided transaction. On the business side are the vast resources that wealthy individuals, firms, and industry associations spend on campaign financing and lobbying to promote their idiosyncratic interests. On the government side are members of Congress who both depend on campaign contributions from well-heeled supporters and are highly susceptible to the influences of well-paid and relentless lobbyists. This dynamic enables a small, but wealthy and influential elite to trade campaign finance and lobbying dollars for privileged advantages that typically emerge as Congressional legislation, targeted exemptions from legislation, advantageous rules drafted by regulatory agencies, preferred access to credit, direct subsidies, preferential tariffs, tax breaks, and protections from prosecution – just to name a few sources of advantage.[30] In short, cronyism

---

[29] When lobbyist effectively corrupt an administration for the benefit of a particular party, they are serving as "corruption entrepreneurs" who are "masters of social network manipulation," according to sociologist Mark Granovetter, who has called such maniputlation "network manipulation." See Mark Granovetter, "The Social Construction of Corruption" in Victor Nee and Richard Swerdling, eds., *On Capitalism*, Stanford University Press, 2007, pp. 152–175.

[30] For economists, crony capitalism is a special type of moneymaking, which they refer to as "rent-seeking." Rent-seekers seek ways to use the political process to transfer resources from others to themselves. The term "rent-seekers" was coined by Anne Kreuger in "The Political Economy of the Rent-Seeking Society," *The American Economic Review*, 64, no. 3, June 1974, pp. 291–303. Lawrence Lessig also refers to the phenomenon of cronyism as a form of "dependency corruption." See *Republic, Lost: How Money Corrupts Congress – and a Plan to Stop It*, Hachette Book Group, 2015, pp. 15–20 and pp. 230–246, for a complete definition and discussion.

entails the capture of government by entrenched interests. It violates one of the essential conditions of democratic capitalism, which is the "separation of power from wealth and so of politics from the economy (and vice versa)."[31]

David Stockman, former director of the Office of Management and Budget under President Ronald Reagan, subsequent Wall Street banker, and critic of contemporary capitalism, characterizes this rent-seeking as "stealing through the public purse in ways that reward the super-rich."[32] Similarly, Charles Koch, the politically active (and notable conservative) CEO of Koch Industries, characterizes crony capitalism as "nothing more than welfare for the rich and powerful."[33] Stockman and Koch are correct: Where cronyism operates, public policy becomes skewed toward the rich and the status quo rather than reflecting the popular will.

Cronyism threatens democratic capitalism when innovation, economic efficiency, market pricing, and equal access to government decision-makers are compromised, and when well-placed persons invest their wealth in lobbying and campaign contributions to ensure that the system continues to work on their behalf. Cronyism becomes blatantly corrupt when instead of accruing wealth from successfully serving customers in competitive markets, wealth comes from simply being powerful. It also becomes corrupt when it undermines integrity in the discharge of duty by public officials. For all these reasons, cronyism compromises the legitimacy of any governance regime claiming to be democratic.

A classic example of crony capitalism at work is the US sugar industry. Domestic sugar producers have long received generous federal support and protection in response to massive lobbying and large-scale campaign contributions. In the heavily lobbied Farm Bill of 2008, for example, Congress increased price support for sugar producers, while reducing support for producers of all other crops. This support effectively guaranteed the price per pound that the government would pay for raw and refined sugar if producers could not profitably sell at prevailing market prices. The legislation also guaranteed US

---

[31] Wolf, *The Crisis of Democratic Capitalism*, p. 29.

[32] David A. Stockman, *The Great Deformation: The Corruption of Capitalism in America*, Public Affairs, 2013. Stockman, budget director in the Reagan administration and an early partner in the Blackstone Group, also refers to crony capitalism as "a mutant regime, which now threatens to cripple the nation's bedrock institutions of political democracy and the free market economy," (p. 3). That mutant regime, according to Stockman, results from a large public budget that offers subsidies and tax breaks to favored firms and a regulatory regime that also favors certain businesses. Stockman's solution is less government rather than more democratic capitalism – a major point of difference with this Element. See Chapter 3, "Days of Crony Capitalism Plunder," pp. 35–52.

[33] Charles G. Koch, "Cronyism Is for the Rich and Powerful" www.wichitaliberty.org/economic-freedom/cronyism-welfare-rich-powerful-writes-charles-koch/.

suppliers of beet and cane sugar 85 percent of the domestic market for human consumption. Because of these price supports and protections – whose annual costs, paid by consumers, is about $3.7 billion according to Agralytica[34] – US sugar prices have been 64–92 percent higher than world prices in recent years.

The big question, of course, is how this highly favorable deal for sugar producers has lasted so long. The answer lies in the industry's political influence. Lobbying by the sugar industry has accounted for more than 33 percent of all funds spent on lobbying by US crop producers – even though sugar production accounts for only 1.9 percent of the value of all US crop production. Donations to political action committees (PACs) from sugar companies also exceeded those of all other US crop producers combined. In 2013, for example, the sugar industry spent about $9 million on lobbying, according to the Center for Responsive Politics, with the top client – American Crystal Sugar – paying about $1.10 million in lobbying fees. Meanwhile, campaign contribution from the industry to Republican and Democratic congressional candidates alike was more than $5 million in 2012, with American Crystal Sugar contributing $2.1 million of that amount.

This story – like comparable ones in the energy, transportation, finance, pharmaceuticals, and manufacturing industries – stands out as an example of crony capitalism. Clearly, Congress and industry players have colluded in formulating a set of policies that serve private interests at the expense of US consumers. Where's the public interest in the sugar industry story? Barely there, other than perhaps preserving farm employment for a very limited number of producers at an enormous public cost. Consumers pay far above world prices for sugar, and the tax-paying public forks over billions of dollars to an industry where, according to the *Wall Street Journal*, just three companies that produce about 20 percent of the US sugar supply receive more than half of the sugar industry price support. Carried interest?

As clear as the sugar industry example of cronyism may be, many relationships in the real world are not always neatly characterized. Most troublesome is that the legitimate public interest or dereliction in matters involving industry subsidies, tax preferences, and legislative loopholes is often difficult to determine.

Take, for example, the case of wind farms. Most wind farms would not be economically viable without a tax credit. When developers of wind energy started receiving a production tax credit in 1992, was that cronyism? Not if the

---

[34] "Economic Effects of the Sugar Program Since the 2008 Farm Bill & Policy Implications for the 2013 Farm Bill," Agralytica, June 3, 2013, https://efaidnbmnnnibpcajpcglclefindmkaj/;https://fairsugarpolicy.org/wordpress/wp-content/uploads/2018/03/AgralyticaEconomicEffectsPaperJune2013.pdf.

federal government wanted to foster energy independence, a new source of clean energy, and a new tool for fighting global warming – all presumably in the public interest, and perhaps justifiable under the general welfare clause of the Constitution (Article, Section 8). Viewed in this light, tax breaks for wind farms escape the taint of cronyism. However, some critics, including Senator Lamar Alexander (R-TN), claimed that the tax breaks unfairly and inappropriately undercut coal and nuclear power, waste money, and promote an industry that "destroy[s] the environment in the name of saving the environment."[35] Senator Alexander was particularly incensed over the fact that the tax credit – then set at 2.3 cents for each kilowatt-hour of wind power produced – was sometimes worth more than the energy it subsidized. In markets such as Texas and Illinois, Alexander claimed that "sometimes ... the subsidy is so large that wind producers have paid utilities to take their electricity and still make a profit." So, is the wind tax credit an example of appropriate national energy policy or a financial windfall for wealthy investors at the expense of the national budget? It depends. In the case of alternate energy production and services, which includes wind farms, private firms spent more than $48 million on lobbying Congress in 2022 for investment tax credits and other incentives, according to Open Secrets, a comprehensive resource for campaign contributions and lobbying data. At the state level, it is not uncommon for lobbying by off-shore wind farms alone to range from $4 to $8 million a year.[36]

Business–government relationships that comprise the toolkit of crony capitalism include (1) campaign financing of elected representatives; (2) heavy lobbying of Congress and other rule-writing agencies of government; and (3) the "revolving door" between government service and the private sector employment, and vice versa. Although these relationships may be perfectly legal, they each represent potential corruptions of democratic capitalism – where business-friendly public policy results from nonrepresentative forces, leading to a diminution of public trust in our leading institutions of business and government.

Ironically, both campaign financing by private citizens and lobbying by business (and nonbusiness) interest groups have historically played a central and often essential role in the functioning of American government. Without the government spending a penny, campaign contributions from individuals, corporations, industry associations, labor unions, and PACs have long funded elections to public office. Similarly, lobbying has long fed costly information

---

[35] Lamar Alexander, "Wind-Power Tax Credits Need to Be Blown Away," *Wall Street Journal*, May 7, 2014, p. A17, https://www.wsj.com/articles/SB10001424052702304547704579561780933591384.

[36] Joe Donohue, "Offshore Wind Power Developers Have Spent Almost $4.2 million on Lobbying during the Past Decade," *New Jersey Globe*, May 3, 2021.

to legislators at no cost to the public. At first blush, this may seem like an efficient arrangement – and one protected by the First Amendment of the US Constitution under the "right to petition" the government. However, when a relatively small group of wealthy individuals and corporations contribute large amounts of undisclosed or "dark money" that becomes the major source of funding for campaign finance budgets, the democratic nature of electoral process is severely compromised. Similarly, when business interests engage in massive lobbying efforts that result in direct quid-pro-quo benefits or crowd out the voice of contending interests before Congress and regulatory agencies, the unequal power of these individuals and firms not only disables the electoral process, but also leads to electoral dropouts and public alienation. This is money that speaks not for ordinary people, but for vested interests, and it has been a problem for a long time. Over a 100 years ago, Republican Senator from Ohio Mark Hanna quipped in 1895: "There are two things important in politics. The first is money, and I can't remember the second."

John Kerry's farewell speech to the Senate on January 30, 2013, after he was confirmed as secretary of state, provides a more considered statement about campaign financing. Speaking about the key challenges facing the Senate based on his twenty-five years in the chamber, Senator Kerry said:

> There is another challenge we must address – and it is the corrupting force of the vast sums of money necessary to run for office. The unending chase for money, I believe, threatens to steal our democracy itself. I've used the word corrupting – and I mean by it not the corruption of individuals, but a corruption of a system itself that all of us are forced to participate in against our will. The alliance of money and the interests it represents, the access it affords those who have it at the expense of those who don't, the agenda it changes or sets by virtue of its power, is steadily silencing the voice of the vast majority of Americans who have a much harder time competing, or who can't compete at all.
>
> The insidious intention of that money is to set the agenda, change the agenda, block the agenda, define the agenda of Washington. How else could we possibly have a U.S. tax code of some 76,000 pages? Ask yourself, how many Americans have their own page, their own tax break, their own special deal?
>
> ... This is what contributes to the justified anger of the American people. They know it. They know we know it. And yet nothing happens. The truth requires that we call the corrosion of money in politics what it is: it is a form of corruption, and it muzzles more Americans than it empowers, and it is an imbalance that the world has taught us can only sow the seeds of unrest.[37]

---

[37] January 30, 2013, www.c-span.org/video/?c4344563/kerry-farewell-speech.

In 2022, according to a CBS News/YouGov, 86 percent of Americans seem to agree with Kerry. Respondents selected the influence of money in politics (among other assorted reasons) as the top reason why our democracy is under threat.[38]

According to OpenSecrets, the total amount of money donated by individuals giving more than $200 (such donations must be reported to the Federal Election Commission (FEC)) and PACs rose from $500 million in the 1990 election cycle to $8.0 billion in 2012 and $16.4 billion in 2020.[39] These numbers have been adjusted for inflation. By the way, Super PAC spending adds another 20 percent to this total.[40]

As with campaign contributions, the scale of congressional lobbying by businesses is large and, by some measures, getting larger. According to OpenSecrets, there were 12,555 registered federal lobbyists in 2023, up from 11,500 in 2014. The total lobbying dollars spent at the federal level in 2023 was $3.1 billion, up from $2.4 billion ten years earlier in nominal dollars.

It should therefore come as no surprise that legislative proposals and policies that wealthy individuals and corporations (owned largely by the economic elite) support have much greater chances of becoming law than those supported by the "average citizen." According to one of most detailed and current studies of which set of actors (such as average citizens, economic elites, and organized interest groups, whether mass-based or business-oriented) have the most influence over public policy, most of the American public has little influence over the policies our government adopts.[41] Take the 2017 tax cut, for example. Prior to the passage of the tax bill, 56 percent of Americans disapproved of the proposed changes to the tax code, according to a Gallup poll. Two years after the tax cut,

---

[38] This survey was conducted with a nationally representative sample of 2085 US adult residents interviewed during August 29–31, 2022. The sample was weighted according to gender, age, race, and education based on the US Census American Community Survey and Current Population Survey, as well as to 2020 presidential vote. The margin of error is ±2.6 points. www.cbsnews.com/news/cbs-news-poll-americans-democracy-is-under-threat-opinion-poll-2022-09-01/.

[39] OpenSecrets data is produced by the Center for Responsive Politics. See www.opensecrets.org/open-data.

[40] In contrast to traditional PACS, Super PACs may raise unlimited sums of money from corporations, unions, organizations, and individuals but are prohibited from donating money directly to political candidates or coordinating with the candidates they support.

[41] Martin Gilens and Benjamin I. Page, "Testing Theories of American Politics: Elites, Interest Groups, and Average Citizens," *Perspectives on Politics*, American Political Science Association, 12, no. 3, September 2014, published online by Cambridge University Press, September 18. www.cambridge.org/core/journals/perspectives-on-politics/article/testing-theories-of-american-politics-elites-interest-groups-and-average-citizens/62327F513959D0A304D4893B382B992B.

only 39 percent of Americans approved of the new law.[42] Rebecca Henderson concludes: "That's not surprising: Most estimates suggest that at least 80% of the benefits from the cut have gone to the wealthiest 10%."[43]

Multiplying the ill effects of vast amounts of money in politics is the so-called revolving door between business and government. This happens when the continuous movement of senior executives and staff between the private sector and public service leads to a shared ideology favoring business interests over the public interest. This phenomenon has been referred to as "regulatory capture," and generations of economists have profiled it.

The financial costs of cronyism's toolkit imposed on Americans and democratic capitalism are large and growing. Many of the direct economic costs – costs stemming from legislation favorable to business, targeted exemptions from otherwise threatening legislation, advantageous rules drafted by regulatory agencies, preferred access to credit, direct subsidies, preferential tariffs, tax breaks, and protections from prosecution – can be crudely estimated. For example, a recent Cato Institute study calculated that the federal government spends almost $100 billion annually on direct and indirect subsidies to small businesses, large corporations, and industry organizations, and this total does not consider tax loopholes and favorable regulatory and trade decisions. Here's the quid pro quo: As already mentioned, industry spending on lobbying alone amounted to $3.1 billion in 2023, a 30 percent increase over the previous decade. According to Pulitzer Prize winner Herrick Smith, the monies financed legions of business lobbyists, which have out-numbered trade union lobbyists in Washington by as much as thirty times and the combined total of labor, consumer, and public interest lobbyists by sixteen times. In dollar terms, this gave business and trade groups nearly a 60-to-1 business advantage in the early decades of the millennium.[44] Other costs – such as the degradation of values such as self-restraint, truthfulness, trustworthiness, and lawfulness that are vital to the functioning of capitalism and democracy and the crumbling of public confidence in the nation's democratic processes and institutions – defy precise quantification but are the most important costs of cronyism over the long run.

---

[42] Megan Brenan, "More Still Disapprove than Approve of 2017 Tax Cuts," October 10, 2018. https://news.gallup.com/poll/243611/disapprove-approve-2017-tax-cuts.aspx.

[43] Rebecca Henderson, "The Business Case for Saving Democracy."

[44] Herrick Smith, *Who Stole the American Dream?* Random House, 2012. Lobbying dollars encompass expenses spent on influencing individual Congresspersons, Congressional committees, and regulatory agencies tasked with developing (often highly contested) implementation guidelines for passed legislation. Agencies can spend years determining the details of how to apply a piece of legislation.

3.2 Democracy's Retreat: Restricted Suffrage

The second deadly cancer attacking democratic capitalism involves the restricted voice and political influence for many ordinary citizens. These restrictions stem from electoral rules and practices that muzzle the voice of ordinary citizens by curbing their rights to run for public office, to vote and express their will on all matters of policy, and to shape their own community as they see fit. US history is littered with episodes of granting and withdrawing voting rights to Black men and women, native Americans, Mexican Americans in the southwest, Chinese Americans, non-English speaking immigrants, and other demographic groups.

Most rules and regulations affecting such voting rights are state-specific, per Article IV of the Constitution.[45] The major exception to this generalization is the Voting Rights Act of 1965, which outlawed discriminatory voting practices adopted in the South after the Civil War and afterward. One of the most discriminatory was the partisan redesign of voting districts to limit the influence of Black voters by shuffling these citizens between districts to maintain the minority share of Black voters in each. This practice is commonly referred to as "redistricting to dilute the African American vote." (Other discriminatory practices included poll taxes, literacy requirements, burdensome photo identification, the closing or moving of polling stations, restrictions on community-based registration drives, and the elimination of same-day registration and early voting.) To remedy this situation, the Voting Rights Act of 1965 was passed and signed by President Lyndon Johnson after numerous peaceful demonstrations by civil rights leaders brought renewed attention to the issue of voting rights. Since 1965, however, various protections of citizens' rights to vote that were spelled out in the Act have been withdrawn by US Supreme Court decisions. Such decisions have had the unfortunate effect of limiting African American voter registration along with their political power. Most significantly, the Supreme Court's decision in *Shelby County* v. *Holder* in 2013 invalidated a key provision of the Voting Rights Act of 1965 that determined the formula by which states and jurisdictions were required to undergo preclearance of any changes in voting law or practices before their implementation. Once the Court struck down this preclearance requirement, Texas and North Carolina

---

[45] Furthermore, constitutional lawyer Richard Hasen pointed out that "the U.S. Constitution contains no affirmative right to vote" as in other democracies such as Canada and Germany. Hasan writes: "The original Constitution provided for voting only for the House of Representatives, leaving voter qualifications for House elections to the states" – all of which was reconfirmed by the Supreme Court in the *Bush* v. *Gore* contested Florisa election case. See Richard L. Hasen, "The U.S. Lacks What Every Democracy Needs," *The New York Times*. January 17, 2024, p. A22.

immediately moved to impose multiple voting restrictions once again, including the discriminatory redesign of voting districts without federal oversight. With these redistricting efforts came a wave of redistricting challenges across the South, and the Act is still being litigated today. What's at stake, of course, is citizens' voice and influence.

For example, over a decade after the *Shelby* v. *Holder* decision, the implementation of the eviscerated Voting Rights Act of 1965 is currently before the Supreme Court. The high court is considering South Carolina's attempt to reinstate a congressional redistricting plan that a lower court found had exiled 30,000 Black voters to create a district safer for a white Republican candidate. The lower court found that South Carolina's mapmakers tried to keep the African American population below a certain target in the Charleston County district, thereby treating it "in a fundamentally different way than the rest of the state."

Wherever universal suffrage and voter representation in a market economy is curtailed by local, state, or federal rules and rulemakers – and citizen voice and influence is thereby isolated or eliminated – the delicate marriage between capitalism and democracy is placed under enormous stress. Laissez-faire capitalism creates many uncertainties and inequalities, which can overwhelm the great majority of the public, which cannot protect or insure itself against the misfortunes that dynamic capitalism can bring. As such, we have seen from consistent public polling that the absence of meaningful political voice and representation in dealing with these matters jeopardizes the perceived legitimacy of our current political economy.

Restricted voice and influence creates another challenge for democratic capitalism – that is, ensuring that political power is accountable to those who depend on it. In the United States, the development of representative democracy over the past 175 years has created the framework for an accountable political system populated by professional politicians who act as intermediaries between the electorate and government bodies and whose re-electability is contingent on representing their constituencies' interests. The weaker the political voice of these constituencies, the less accountability these intermediaries have and the less democratic our system of economic and political governance becomes. This is the direction we are headed today, and, as we have seen, the public is beginning to feel serious anxiety.

It is no secret that two major factors are contributing to this anxiety and restricted political voice in the US setting: (1) ballot access for prospective candidates and (2) accessible voting for those who want to register their voice in local, state, and national elections. Because most election rules, practices, and behaviors are state-specific, it makes sense to start addressing these two factors on a state-specific basis, such as in my home state of Massachusetts.[46] Many other states could provide salient examples of highly cynical political theatre dealing with increased restrictions on political voice and influence – all in the name of protecting the integrity of suffrage.

With respect to ballot access, state laws define the scope of voter choice – and the variety of ways states can restrict ballot access is mindboggling. For democracy to function, however, every viable candidate should be able to compete, and every election should meaningfully reflect diverse viewpoints. This is clearly not the case across the country, however, because numerous states design their primaries to prevent viable candidates from running for office.

For example, under Florida state law, if a party only signs off on one candidate for the primary ballot, the primary contest is not held. Citing this law, the state Democratic party refused to put Rep. Dean Phillips (D-Minnesota) on the state's primary ballot in November 2023. This denied Phillips the chance to compete against President Biden in the Democratic primary election for that party's 2024 presidential nomination. This is clear example of America's dysfunctional primary election system in action.

Massachusetts has its own set of idiosyncrasies and dysfunctions. Such characteristics resulted in the state running, after the 2020 election cycle, the least competitive legislative election among all states, judging by the number of open elections, contested primaries, and contested general elections. According to Partners in Democracy, a nonprofit committed to renovating institutions of democracy, Democrats had primary choices in just 20 percent of state legislative seats in either chamber, whereas Republicans had a primary choice in just 5 percent of Senate and 1.25 percent of House seats.[47] This extremely low level of primary choices and lack of competition for seats in the state legislature suggests that ballot access at nominating conventions for new, relatively unknown candidates was restricted by both party rules and the power of incumbency.

Here's how these restrictions work. To get on a Democratic or Republican primary ballot for electoral office in Massachusetts, candidates must first collect

---

[46] In addition to these two restrictions on political voice, a strong argument can be made that the current, unrepresentative size of the US House of Representatives also impinges on the exercise of citizens' political voice. Danielle Allen, who cochaired the American Academy of Arts and Sciences Commission on the State of Our Democracy, has written extensively on this subject. She has argued that increasing the size of the House would help the United States achieve more inclusive, responsive, and energetic governance, while reconnecting House members to their constituents and enabling members to better understand and represent their constituents' voice. See, for example, "How Big Should the House Be? Let's Do the Math," *The Washington Post*, March 28, 2023. https://wapo.st/3qlYNZP.

[47] https://partnersindemocracy.us.

10,000 signatures and second, win at least 15 percent of delegates' votes at party nominating conventions. For Democrats, the required 15 percent of convention delegates' votes is tallied by a winner-take-all rule, which means in a primary race against an incumbent with significant name recognition, it is difficult for a newcomer to gain a majority of precinct votes in a first run for office. Normally, we would celebrate a newcomer getting, say, 25 percent of a precinct's vote. But, in Massachusetts, if an incumbent with a reasonable reputation gathers 30 percent of a precinct's votes, it is winner-take-all and the so-called successful newcomer is totally vanquished and takes no votes to the nominating convention to count toward his or her qualifying 15 percent of convention votes. This procedure results in weakly contested or uncontested primaries and almost a blockade against new candidates representing new ideas and constituencies. According to Ballotpedia, which tracks elections nationally, Massachusetts was rated in 2022 as the least competitive state in the country based on factors such as how often an incumbent faces a challenger – and this has been the case in at least the past three election cycles.[48] As just one example, Congressional incumbents in Massachusetts have lost a seat only twice in the last twenty-seven years.[49]

Many other states besides Massachusetts field uncompetitive elections. According to No Labels, a political action group committed to restoring faith in American democracy, only 36 out of 435 House general elections were truly competitive in 2022 – where "competitive" is defined as one that is decided by five points or less. There have been fewer and fewer of these races every year.[50]

Another significant result of the current candidate selection system is that candidate diversity is very low for certain populations. For example, the percentage of people of color in the Massachusetts state legislature and legislative leadership are, respectively, barely 10 percent and 5 percent, way below the 20 percent share of population in the state. And in seven of the state's ten largest

---

[48] "Primary election competitiveness in state and federal government, 2022," https://ballotpedia .org/Primary_election_competitiveness_in_state_and_federal_government,_2022#Massa chusetts.

[49] Matt Stout, "Blue Mass: Changing Its Colors," *The Boston Globe*, October 12, 2023, p. 1.

[50] This claim has been substantiated and elaborated by Fix Our House, an education and advocacy group promoting proportional representation as an urgently needed electoral reform. In a study of the 2022 House general election, Fix Our House found that only 42 of 435 House elections were competitive in 2022 (again measured by margins of victory), and that 35 House seats were uncontested. Of these uncontested thirty-five races, the study reported that nineteen districts only had one major party candidate on the ballot. This finding was partly due to the fact that many voters do not live in evenly divided communities and partly due to "successful" redistricting or gerrymandering of voters by political parties. See Lauren Sforza, "Only 10 Percent of House Races Were Competitive in Midterms: Advocacy Group," *The Hill*, March 23, 2023, https:// thehill.com/homenews/campaign/3897518-only-10-percent-of-house-races-were-competitive- in-midterms-advocacy-group/.

cities, people of color make up a smaller share of the City Council than their population. According to FairVote, a nonpartisan organization seeking better elections, Massachusetts was ranked tenth in its assessment of the nineteen worst ballot access laws in the United States and joins a large number of states with the most restrictive ballot access regimes in the nation.[51]

With respect to accessible voting, the record in Massachusetts is mixed. On the plus side, there is permanent vote-by-mail and in-person early voting. On the negative side, there is no universal automatic voter registration (available in fourteen other states); no same-day registration (available in nineteen other states); no electronic voting (available in four states and DC); and election day is not a holiday, so many voters must take time off work to vote many times a year. We know that any restrictions on citizens' right to vote naturally affects total voter turnout.

Turnout in Massachusetts state primaries has seen wide fluctuations, but the state has seen a general decline to below 20 percent until a jump upward during the Trump years. In presidential primaries, except for the Trump years, voter turnout in Massachusetts has not exceeded 50 percent since 1952. (According to FairVote, voter turnout in the United States is much lower than in other countries, hovering around 60 percent in presidential elections and 40 percent in midterm election years. Turnout soars to 90 percent in countries with mandatory voting and reaches around 70 percent in other developed countries.)

Possibly due to restricted ballot access and the lack of candidate diversity, Massachusetts was forty-eighth in the country for the gap between white and people of color voter turnout in 2020. Black turnout was 36 percent, just over half of white turnout. Black, Latinex, and Asian American and Pacific Islander (AAPI) voters as a group cast 13.3 percent of votes in 2022, while accounting for 26.3 percent of the state's population.

Adding fuel to the fire of restricted political voice is a lack of legislative and administrative transparency in Massachusetts and other states. Lack of transparency makes it difficult for voters to see the policy implications of their electoral choices. According to Partners in Democracy, many issues contribute here. As just one example, Massachusetts does not require committee votes and often does not require floor votes (to get a floor vote, sixteen representatives must demand it); the legislature often waits until the very end of the session to complete business, leading to rushed processes with limited potential for public oversight. Furthermore, the lack of public voting records makes it difficult to discern the positions of individual legislators. In a democracy, the lack of public

---

[51] https://fairvote.org/the_primary_problem_with_american_primaries_lack_of_competition/.

sector transparency effectively disables public voice and influence, especially with respect to institutionalized cronyism.

It is poor news for democratic capitalism if the Massachusetts experience indicates the variety of restrictions on political voice throughout the fifty states. A weak or unhealthy democracy is not a boon to market capitalism. Where the people's voice is neither heard nor represented – thereby freeing the political governance regime from rigorous oversight and control – the economic and political sustainability of democratic capitalism is inevitably compromised. In the absence of democratic feedback over both formulating and implementing legislated rules and policies that affect decision-making by independent economic actors, the probabilities that a market economy based on private property rights will behave in ways that can serve both public and private interests will decline rapidly. In one credible scenario, cronyism in its various forms might become even more malignant than it is today, thereby exposing democratic capitalism to a further loss in public confidence and trust.

4 Restoring the Promise of Democratic Capitalism

The death grip of cronyism (on one side) and restricted political voice (on the other) represent an unsustainable imbalance of power in our political economy. So, the big question facing us is whether or not the idea of democratic capitalism can serve as a realistic aspiration or illuminating ideal for the United States going forward. The answer is this: not without a lot of remedial work.

To make progress in unlocking this death grip of opposing constituencies, we first need to agree on basic principles of democratic action that can curb the excesses of American-style cronyism and strengthen the political voice and influence of ordinary citizens who are affected by the ill-effects of cronyism and other forms of domination. We then need to demonstrate how these principles can be usefully applied to (1) containing the curse of cronyism, (2) strengthening political voice and suffrage, and, to add another precondition, and (3) promoting the appeal and presence of democracy-supporting firms in our political economy.

We also need a moral culture that supports a political system striving to be more democratic and more representative of citizens' preferences. I address this cultural condition in Section 6.

4.1 Political Equality as a Guiding Principle

There is no rational way to expect enduring support for any intended democratic activity if the principle of political equality is not baked into that activity. This is as true for democratic capitalism as it is for democracy itself. This is because political equality is such a central value of the democratic aspiration.

According to philosopher and democracy advocate Danielle Allen, the principle of political equality follows from the fundamental concept of human moral equality. Moral equality refers to our basic need to be an autonomous, purposeful author of our lives and to have that need and personal capacity "recognized as a necessary element of well-being, worth, and dignity."[52] In a complex society, the only way for us to be maximally autonomous and purposeful is to be cocreators or active participants in creating the societal constraints that bound our lives – and to be free from domination by other individuals or groups in this participation. In everyday life, this individual freedom includes "meaningful participation in collective decision-making" related to matters such as cultural practices, the structure of civil society, and participating in the institutions of political governance.[53] The freedom and capability of doing this defines the essence of political equality.

Political equality should not be confused with economic equality, social equality, or gender equality, although each of these are important.[54] As suggested, political equality means personal autonomy, freedom from domination, access to the institutions of government such as legislative and regulatory bodies, and the ability to shape one's own life and community. The term "political" in this context refers to being involved in a governance system in which participants typically have nonidentical interests. This involvement is two-faced. One face is the conduct of governing bodies, whether in the public sector or private sector. The other face relates to the members' standing and freedoms within these governing bodies as they participate in aspects of institutional governance that affect their lives. In this sense, political equality relates to egalitarian participation in the institutions of civil society on matters that affect one's current welfare and future possibilities.

Whereas political equality is a shared value or organizing principle, it provides the intellectual framework to protect two important categories of rights: (1) *individual* rights related to free speech and association, freedom of religion, freedom to choose one's employment, property ownership, as well as the right to be left alone and to commit one's personal property in commercial transactions in ways that serve one's own well-being and (2) *collective* rights related to the freedom to participate in politics as a voter, elected official, and decision-maker in political institutions. Democracy, according to Allen, is the only governance system that can guarantee both these categories of rights

---

[52] Allen, *Justice by Means of Democracy*, p. 32.   [53] Ibid., p. 33.   [54] Ibid., p. 32.

and, in doing so, guarantee the existence of political equality itself.[55] I acknowledge Allen's work here because it succinctly explains why the democratic component of capitalism as an economic governance system is so important to preserve.

It is also worth noting that political equality, or at least the promise of political equality, is a central feature of American political and constitutional theory. However, while a succession of court cases (such as the US Supreme Court's 1954 landmark decision in *Brown* v. *Board of Education*) and legislation (such as the Voting Rights Act of 1965) have affirmed political equality as a foundation of American liberty,[56] there is still a large gap between theory and practice when it comes to campaign finance. For example, when the Supreme Court found in *Citizens United* v. *Federal Election Commission* (2010) judged that a federal law prohibiting corporations and unions from making expenditures in connection with federal elections was unconstitutional, it had the effect of limiting political equality – by limiting "the right of Americans to participate and be represented in our political system on equal terms – regardless of wealth or class" in national elections.[57] This is because when money from corporations and other wealthy players come to have a dominant impact on policy, many Americans are no longer equal citizens when participating in the political process. I return to Citizens United below.

Other than these constitutional matters, the daily implementation of political equality – with its emphasis on nondomination, equal access to the instruments of government, and participative problem-solving on matters affecting one's well-being – relies on various forms of reciprocity and power sharing. As I discuss next, reciprocity or mutual responsiveness anchors the principle of political equality in a contentious world, where progress requires compromise and negotiation, as well as the recognition and reciprocation of sacrifices made by some members of the polity on behalf of others.[58] Political equality, along with reciprocity and nondomination as critical subprinciples, enables inclusive deliberation and problem-solving by parties with often conflicting interests. This is a form of governance that does not exist under other forms of capitalism, including state-guided capitalism, welfare capitalism, or autocratic (oligarchic) capitalism.

---

[55] Ibid., p. 33. For an informative, historical review of philosophical discussions pertaining to major categories of individual rights, see pp. 20–30.

[56] Jeffrey D. Clements, "But It Will Happen": A Constitutional Amendment to Secure Political Equality in Election Spending and Representation, *Harvard Law & Policy Review*, 13, 2019, pp. 394, 397.

[57] Ibid., pp. 398–399.   [58] Allen, *Justice by Means of Democracy*, p. 42.

4.2 Containing Cronyism

The most evocative example of the lack of political equality – and of domination and the lack of equal access to the instruments of government – is cronyism. Consider, for example, two major tools in the toolkit of crony capitalism: campaign financing and political lobbying. Cronyism is a serious problem when well-placed and influential parties invest individual and corporate wealth in lobbying and political contributions to ensure that the political system works on their behalf, even if it retards innovation and economic efficiency. This is a clear form of economic and political domination of those without the means to play the big money game in politics. In addition, it is a prime example of how access to the instruments of government can be blocked for those without the benefit of a political war chest of comparable size.

Numerous self-evident reforms can help contain the damage that cronyism imposes on democratic capitalism. To start, we can push for greater transparency, including better reporting of industry and business lobbying on specific pieces of legislation and regulatory rulewriting. At minimum, the public would have greater clarity about who is bringing how much fire power to legislative rulemaking and regulatory rulefollowing. Federal law – principally the Lobbying Disclosure Act of 1995 and the Honest Leadership and Open Government Act of 2007 – does not now require such disclosure. This needs to change. Reporting all corporate political activities should be made mandatory. Not only would this bring greater transparency in how companies exercise political influence, but it would also allow investors, employees, and customers to judge consistency among companies' publicly espoused values and actual lobbying behavior on matters ranging from clean air standards to tax policy.

We can also strengthen restrictions on the revolving door. President Obama did this with one of his first executive orders, which prohibited former lobbyists from working at agencies and on issues they had previously lobbied, and which barred them altogether from related advisory boards and commissions. In addition, we can tighten requirements for cooling-off periods for public- and private-sector officials passing through the revolving door to minimize trust-destroying conflicts of interest and privileged access by influential business interests to Congress and regulatory agencies.

While both initiatives would be extremely useful and should be pursued, no significant containment or reversal of American-style crony capitalism will occur without a major change in our approach to campaign financing. As Robert Kaiser, an experienced political reporter and editor of the *Washington Post* argued in *So Damn Much Money* (2009), lobbying has not only corroded

American government but also has interfered with the legislative agenda of both the Right and the Left.

Our country has a long history of attempted campaign finance reform, starting with the Tilman Act of 1907, which prohibited corporations and nationally chartered (interstate) banks from making direct financial contributions to federal candidates. The act was an early attempt to reduce the power and influence of large banks on congressional and presidential elections, but unfortunately weak enforcement undercut the act's potential effectiveness. Much more recently, Congress has crafted legislation such as the Bipartisan Campaign Reform Act of 2002, also called the McCain-Feingold Act. As succinctly explained by OpenSecrets in "The Legacy and Impact of McCain-Feingold," this act was written to prohibit soft money contributions to national political parties, and to limit campaign financing in hard money.[59] (Soft money is unlimited funding collected by political parties intended for party strengthening, whereas hard money is donations made directly to a candidate's campaign.) Opponents of the McCain-Feingold Act successfully argued eight years later in the *Citizens United* case that the law would be a restraint on the freedom of corporations, unions, and wealthy individuals to express themselves. Following *Citizens United*, parties were free to spend money independently either supporting or opposing individual candidates, and the path was cleared for individuals and corporations to contribute unlimited amounts, mostly undisclosed or shielded through shell companies, as long as they were not working with campaigns and political parties. Within two years of the *Citizens United* decision, about 85 percent of funding for congressional campaigns came from large contributors – mainly wealthy individuals and corporations – with a negative effective on American democracy.[60] In addition, according to the Brennan Center for Justice at New York University, this Supreme Court decision led to the creation of Super PACs that "empower the wealthiest donors, and the expansion of dark money through shadowy nonprofits that don't disclose their donors."[61] Whereas traditional PACs raise and spend money in support of, or in opposition to, political candidates, legislation, or ballot initiatives, and are limited to raising a maximum of $3,300 per year per candidate per election, Super PACs have no such spending limit and can accept unlimited contributions from individuals and corporations as long as they don't contribute to the

---

[59] Kaitlin Washburn, "The Legacy and Impact of McCain-Feingold," *OpenSecrets*, posted August 28, 2018. www.opensecrets.org/news/2018/08/the-legacy-of-mccain-feingold.

[60] See Lawrence Lessig, *Republic, Lost*. In his public statements, Lessign refers to the *Citizens United* decision as "the decision that broke democracy."

[61] Tim Lau, "Citizen United Explained," *Brennan Center for Justice*. www.brennancenter.org/our-work/research-reports/citizens-united-explained?ref=foreverwars.ghost.io.

campaigns of individual candidates. Super PACs do have some disclosure requirements on the books, but because many of these donors contribute through groups that are difficult to identify, the original source of these donations – referred to as "dark money" – are often unclear.[62]

What this means is that a tiny group of largely unidentified contributors can affect the policy agenda of Congress and block reforms of all kinds. According to an analysis by political scientists Martin Gilens of Princeton and Benjamin Page of Northwestern University, "Economic elites and organized groups representing business interests have substantial independent impacts on U.S. government policy, while average citizens and mass-based interest groups have little or no independent influence."[63] This is truly a picture of domination by an American oligarchy and, correspondingly, the denial of equal access to the instruments of government.

Unfortunately, the long and contorted history of attempted campaign finance reform sends a clear message: It is next to impossible for incumbent members of Congress to agree on meaningful controls on funds flowing into federal elections. More meaningful controls would of course lessen the probability of incumbents being elected. Most party leaders, and more than a few legal scholars and the current Supreme Court, oppose controls that would diminish the role of money in politics, arguing that controls would be "an infringement on free speech and healthy political competition." Such intransigence in Congress and the Supreme Court leaves only a few paths forward for reforming the status quo: repealing *Citizens United* (through a constitutional amendment), broadening the donor disclosure requirements of Super PACs that currently serve as the principal channel of dark money to political campaigns of all sorts, and/or changing the financing opportunities for political campaigns in ways that strengthen voters' voice and curb the coercive impact of unregulated money in politics.

With respect to taking the *Citizens United* decision off the books through constitutional amendment, such a strategy faces a very high hurdle for success – even though more than 75 percent of Americans appear to favor such an amendment.[64] Amending the US Constitution requires two supermajority votes: a two-thirds vote in both the House and Senate and ratification by three-quarters of state legislatures. According to historian Jill Lapore, who has documented thousands of failed constitutional amendments, this high bar for

---

[62] Ibid.

[63] Gilens and Page, "Testing Theories of American Politics: Elites, Interest Groups, and Average Citizens."

[64] According to American Promise – a national, non-partisan, grassroots organization that advocates for just such a constitutional reform. See https://americanpromise.net/our-plan/.

a constitutional amendment has become even higher since the 1970s "chiefly due to widening political polarization" – making the constitution "effectively un-amendable" today.[65]

Despite the serious political and procedural problems involved in passing an amendment that would annul *Citizen United*, the work of American Promise – a national, nonpartisan, grassroots organization that advocates for just such a constitutional reform – has been able to show substantial progress in building a movement aimed at implementing constitutional reform through a full range of civic actions: by recruiting proselytizing volunteers, signing petitions, gathering ballot signatures, voting on resolutions, visiting representatives, presenting to Rotary Clubs and local Chambers of Commerce, writing letters to the editor, commenting on social media, setting up tables at farmers' markets or wherever Americans gather to discuss opportunities for change, and so on. As a result, the legislatures of twenty-two states have passed bipartisan "ready-to-ratify" resolutions calling for an amendment to the US Constitution that would provide states with authority to regulate campaign financing.[66]

As currently drafted by American Promise, such a constitutional amendment (it would be the twenty-eighth) would advance democratic self-government and political equality by enabling states to regulate and "set reasonable limits on the raising and spending of money by candidates and others to influence elections ... and may distinguish between natural persons and corporations or other artificial entities created by the law, including by prohibiting such entities from spending money to influence elections."[67] The distinction between "natural persons" and "artificial entities created by law" is critical to the drafting of this amendment, which aims to repair the First Amendment protecting free speech by enabling states to prohibit corporations from directly or indirectly spending money to influence elections and drown out the voices of individual citizens.

Whether or not this amendment initiative will succeed is unclear. Certainly the language of any amendment would undergo deep review and debate in the House and Senate, and many prior attempts at passing amendments of this kind have not survived Congressional debate.[68] Thus, while the current amendment

---

[65] https://amendmentsproject.org.

[66] https://americanpromise.net/campaign-finance-roundup-march-22-2024/.

[67] See Clements, "But It Will Happen": A Constitutional Amendment to Secure Political Equality in Election Spending and Representation, p. 412.

[68] According to Jill Lapore, more than 10,000 proposals to amend the Constitution have been introduced by members of Congress since 1789, and only twenty-seven amendments have been ratified. See Lapore, "The United States' Unamendable Constitution," *The New Yorker*, October 26, 2022.

initiative works toward Congressional review, we need to look at reforming Super PACs and introducing new campaign financing options as two additional avenues for change.

Super PACs, in the aftermath of the *Citizens United* decision, have come to play an outsized role in corrupting democracy. As noted, traditional PACs – which are regulated heavily by the FEC – may accept up to $3,300 in individual contributions to fund campaigns for or against candidates, ballot initiatives, or legislation. Corporations and unions are barred from contributing to such PACs. In marked contrast, Super PACs, which have flourished since *Citizen United*, are allowed to raise unlimited sums of money from corporations, unions, associations, and individuals and then donate unlimited sums to advance the interests of political parties as long as this spending is not coordinated with the campaigns of specific candidates. In practice, the dividing line between coordinated and uncoordinated political contributions can be murky, such as when the Super PACS most closely dedicated to supporting Obama and Romney in the 2012 election cycle were run, respectively, by former aides to the president and his Republican challenger.[69] In the words of the non-partisan Campaign Legal Center, candidates and Super PACs with preferred messaging and other materials to support their campaigns, and contracting through common vendors that are familiar with the candidate's messaging and strategic objectives."[70]

According to Equal Citizens – a nonprofit founded by Lawrence Lessig to fix democracy by establishing truly equal citizenship – the rise of Super PACs as a major campaign finance instrument is one of the leading reasons that our representative democracy has become so corrupt. In the words of Lessig, "the only voices that our government listens to are the special interests who fund their campaigns" and the result is a system of economic and political governance that is "rigged to favor the powerful and the well-connected."[71]

One path forward in curbing this corruption is to activate states to pass anti-Super PAC initiatives that the Supreme Court can then review with petitioners arguing that the federal government indeed has the power to regulate (unlimited) corporate spending on elections, ballot initiatives, and legislation and that *Citizen United* was incorrect in deciding the negative. (This is the strategy Equal Citizens is following in the State of Maine.)

---

[69] ABC News, "What Is a Super PAC? A Short History," https://abcnews.go.com/Politics/OTUS/super-pac-short-history/story?id=16960267.

[70] Sophia Gonsalves-Brown, "Super PAC Deals Are a Bad Deal for Democracy," https://campaignlegal.org/update/super-pac-deals-are-bad-deal-democracy.

[71] Lawrence Lessig at https://equalcitizens.us/about-equal-citizens/.

A parallel path would involve greater disclosure of corporate political spending under an SEC rule requiring such disclosures.[72] Such a disclosure requirement would include disclosure of donations to Super PACs. The last effort to legislate disclosure – the DISCLOSE Act proposed by Representative Chris Van Hollen of Maryland and Senator Chuck Schumer of New York in 2010 – lost by one vote in the House and two votes in the Senate. Since 2011, when a group of law professors proposed that the SEC require mandatory disclosure of corporations' political contributions, the agency has resisted making any decision regarding this hotly debated matter – even though recent polling shows that as many as 80 percent of Americans think it is very/somewhat important for companies to disclose their political donations and lobbying.[73] Another poll reports that two-thirds of self-identified Democrats, Independents, and Republicans support disclosure of political funding.[74] In our current world of undisclosed – or minimal voluntarily disclosed – political contributions, OpenSecrets has calculated that $1 billion in dark money was spent on political campaigns alone in the 2020 election cycle.[75]

Today, the antidemocratic effects of *Citizens United* and the reporting loopholes for Super PACs created in the wake of *Citizens United* remain in place and seem unlikely to be addressed by direct Congressional action. As a result, the FEC has been unable to protect the voice and influence of ordinary voters. Fortunately, however, while the federal government is mired in denial and dysfunction regarding essential democracy reforms, as many as twenty-one states are currently taking actions to expose dark and special interest money in election campaigns.[76] These state-led actions can serve as both an inspiration and legislative model for Congress in designing and passing legislation dealing not only with enhanced disclosure of how corporations spend their political

---

[72] Lucian A. Bebchuk, Robert J. Jackson, Jr., James D. Nelson, and Roberto Tallarita, "The Untenable Case for Keeping Investors in the Dark," *Harvard Business Law Review*, Vol. 10, 2019.

[73] Shannon Cabral, Daniel Krasner, and Rachel Doubledee, "Calls for Transparency around Corporate Political Spend Are Growing Louder," *Just Capital*, May 2, 2023. https://justcapital.com/news/31-percent-of-americas-largest-companies-disclose-lobbying-political-contributions/. See also Ciara Torres-Spelliscy, "More Shareholders Seek Transparency on Corporate Political Spending and Climate Change," Brennan Center for Justice. See www.brennancenter.org/our-work/analysis-opinion/more-shareholders-seek-transparency-corporate-political-spending-and.

[74] Hedrick Smith, Executive Editor of Reclaim the American Dream, "Dark Money: Outing Donors State by State," https://reclaimtheamericandream.org/progress-disclose/.

[75] Anna Massoglia and Karl Evers-Hillstrom, "'Dark Money' Topped $1 Billion in 2020, Largely Boosting Democrats," *Open Secrets*, March 17, 2021, www.opensecrets.org/news/2021/03/one-billion-dark-money-2020-electioncycle/.

[76] See https://reclaimtheamericandream.org/progress-disclose/ for a state-by-state summary.

contributions but also with the disclosure by Super PACs of where contributions from corporations and other wealthy donors are coming from. Broadening these state-level initiatives needs to be the focus of all democracy renovators and proponents of democratic capitalism as a governance ideal.

Turning from Super PAC reform to innovative campaign financing options, many deserve to be tested in practice. One option is a voucher program (as adopted in Seattle in 2015) where voters receive monetary vouchers worth, say, $25 or $250 that can be donated to candidates participating in such a program. Vouchers can provide a simple way to help a more diverse pool of candidates run for office and somewhat reduce the impact of large contributions from wealthy individuals and corporations.

Another option, with similar goals and effects in mind, involves the government providing "matching funds" for the first chunk of donations (say, $250) that private individuals make to a candidate running in a federal election. Matching funds would make small donations more valuable to a campaign, create an incentive for campaigns to pursue such donations, reduce the candidates' and incumbents' dependence on larger gifts from influential wealthy donors, and thereby enhance the power of less-wealthy individuals.

Lawrence Lessig notes that the cost of "voting with dollars"-type reforms would be very small relative to the cost of "corporate welfare" (government subsidies, tax loopholes, and the like), which the Cato Institute, cited previously, calculates to run at about $100 billion a year.[77]

Another approach to campaign finance reform has recently emerged with the swift and ironic rise of so-called independent Super PACs aimed at electing a Congress committed to small-dollar campaign funding.[78] As an example, look at the record of Mayday, a crowd-funded, nonpartisan Super PAC Lessig launched in 2014, which quickly raised $12 million in less than three months to back Congressional candidates who support campaign finance reform.[79] Other super PACs aiming to reduce the influence of wealthy interests and elevate the impact of small donors on campaigns include Counterpace, Friends of Democracy, and Every Voice Action (formerly Friends of Democracy). These initiatives – which targeted specific races and candidates as far back as ten years ago – are the most direct and professionally managed efforts to date aimed at changing the big-money-in-elections game. The failure of such initiatives to gain momentum – against the backdrop of significant legislative failures during the 1990s and the Supreme Court's *Citizen's United*

---

[77] Lessig, *Republic, Lost*, p. 269.
[78] ABC News, "What Is a Super PAC? A Short History," https://abcnews.go.com/Politics/OTUS/super-pac-short-history/story?id=16960267.
[79] Disclosure: The author contributed to the Mayday PAC in 2016.

decision – would be a setback for US democracy and perpetuate the damage cronyism created to democratic capitalism.

Oddly enough, the current structure of campaign finance and lobbying is sometimes explained as a rational attempt by rationally self-interested individuals and institutions to reduce the uncertainties of their world by trying to influence, control, and, wherever possible, dominate political processes affecting their future. All the economic incentives push wealthy and powerful individuals and firms in this direction. But these incentives and resulting behaviors lead to a blatantly nondemocratic outcome: where the nonsacrificeable democratic principles of political equality and nondomination are violated systematically – to the disadvantage of less-well-resourced members of the body politic. What's required to restore the democracy portion of democratic capitalism – before it's too late to reverse the alarming decline in citizen confidence in, and support for, our current governance regime – are the kinds of campaign finance and lobbying reforms suggested here.

4.3 Expanding Political Voice and Influence

There can be no clearer constraint on political voice and influence – and no clearer violation of the core democratic principle of political equality – than the combined effect of limited ballot access, closed primaries, and restrictions limiting accessible voting. As already discussed, where there are high barriers to representative candidates gaining access to ballots, such as highly partisan primaries that exclude nonparty candidates from running for public office and conditions inhibiting the physical casting of votes, large numbers of citizens will be excluded from the electoral process and therefore the political process. This happens, in fact, in many states across the nation, including my home state of Massachusetts.

Political parties control access to primary ballots, and the general public has little ability to modify party rules (especially in states such as Massachusetts, where 61 percent of registered voters are not affiliated with any political party). The most practical approach to rehabilitating our dysfunctional primary election system, therefore, is to open ballot access to first-time and nonparty affiliated candidates – thereby creating more competitive elections – by replacing party primaries with nonpartisan primaries, as Louisiana, California, Washington, and Alaska have already done. A ballot access system such as this is often referred to as a "Top 5" election system, encompassing an "all-comers preliminary" followed by a final election for the Top 5 finishers in that preliminary.

Here's how this electoral innovation would work in state-wide elections as explained by Partners in Democracy, an organization devoted to democracy innovation.[80]

> All candidates running in each election would appear on a single ballot, regardless of whether they are registered with a party. The top 5 finishers in that preliminary election – i.e., the five candidates with the most popular support across the electorate – would then compete in a final election, using 'instant runoff' to ensure that the winner crosses the threshold of winning a majority. This final election would thus feature up to five viable, popular candidates – in contrast to today's elections, which often fail to produce more than one.

This instant runoff system is often referred to as "ranked choice voting."

Under a Top 5 or ranked choice voting system, voters rank the competing candidates by preference. If a candidate wins a majority of first-preference votes, they are declared the winner. If no candidate secures a majority, the candidate with the fewest first-place votes is eliminated, and their votes are transferred to the next choice on each ballot. A new tally is conducted to determine whether any candidate has won a majority of the adjusted votes. The process is repeated until a candidate wins an outright majority.

Such a reform would also foster legislative bodies that better represent the diversity of their constituencies. It prevents wasted votes and re-empowers the broad electorate, instead of the extreme base (which tends to dominate primary elections). Furthermore, independent voters finally get a voice. There is no better way to apply the principle of political equality to the problem of political voice and influence than such an electoral innovation at both the state and municipality levels, as in my hometown, the City of Cambridge.

The standard of political equality also applies to the exercise of citizens' right to vote. In the state of Massachusetts, the exercise of that right is among the lowest in the nation. For example, as recently as 2020, Partners in Democracy reports that Massachusetts was fiftieth in the country for Black voter registration, with only 42 percent of Black Massachusetts residents registered to vote (according to US census data) – the lowest rate of any ethnic group, anywhere in the country recorded in the data that year. As of 2022, Massachusetts continued to be below average in registration rates for Asian American and Hispanic voters. One explanation for this low level of voter turnout is the absence of candidates that appeal to this segment of the electorate. Due to restrictions on ballot access and low voter turnout, Massachusetts has among the fewest

---

[80] Disclosure: The author is Treasurer of Partners in Democracy.

contested elections in the country, which in turn leads to the lack of account-ability and a low level of responsiveness among office holders.

With respect to citizen voting rights, the two most impactful reforms are (1) same-day voter registration and (2) automatic mailing of ballots. Currently, in states such as Massachusetts, citizens must register to vote at least twenty days before an election, which means two trips during a work week for new voters, which creates a barrier for many workers with fixed job schedules. It also creates a barrier for eligible young people in school or university and more transient populations. In brief, this arbitrary restriction keeps thousands of otherwise qualified residents from participating in our democracy. Same- day voter registration would allow unregistered but eligible voters to show up at a polling location on election day or during early voting hours, register, and vote all at the same time. It is already in place in twenty-one states and Washington, DC, and has been working well for more than forty years in states such as Maine and Minnesota. In these states, it has shown to improve voter participation by up to seven points, with an even greater impact in low-income, Black, and Hispanic communities.

Automatic mail-in ballot systems require that election officials automatically send mail-in ballots to all eligible voters – who can then return their ballots by mail or via designated drop boxes. This type of system also boosts voter turnout by expanding voting accessibility, especially among Black and brown people, disabled people, rural residents, older people, and members of the military. Historically, Republicans and Democrats have agreed that this system offers the easiest way to cheat in an election process. But the experience of the nine states allowing mail-in ballots shows that few people have been charged, in fact, for either mail ballot fraud or assistance fraud in elections in which tens of millions of votes were cast.[81]

Same-day voter registration and automatic mailing of ballots are two reforms that would increase levels of voter registration; minimize disparities in voting rates between the suburbs and gateway cities; make it easier for citizens to enter the political process and exercise their influence on matters that affect their lives; and increase citizen's sense that the core democratic value of political equality is not being sabotaged by political and economic elites.

---

[81] According to CNN Fact Check www.cnn.com/factsfirst/politics/factcheck_8b1382ba-4b0e-4d9c-b933-adcbced94e98 and Elise Viebeck, "Minuscule Number of Potentially Fraudulent Ballots in States with Universal Mail Voting Undercuts Trump Claims about Election Risks," *The Washington Post*, June 8, 2020 www.washingtonpost.com/politics/minuscule-number-of-potentially-fraudulent-ballots-in-states-with-universal-mail-voting-undercuts-trump-claims-about-election-risks/2020/06/08/1e78aa26-a5c5-11ea-bb20-ebf0921f3bbd_story.html.

5 Can Firms Become More Democracy-Supporting?

So far, I have not yet addressed the question of how the management of firms affects public (and employee) perceptions of democratic capitalism. I have concentrated instead on behavior affecting, for better or worse, the democratic characteristics of our economic and political markets.

Let's now assume that the adoption of political equality as a central governance principle, enabled by the deft use of power sharing, helps us loosen the stranglehold of cronyism and restricted political voice on US democratic capitalism. If successfully applied in curbing cronyism and restoring universal suffrage, we would still be left with the inconsistency of private sector firms employing millions of people in essentially nondemocratic regimes where the decision hierarchies are administered in ways that are rarely compatible with core democratic principles – where employees lack voice and influence on corporate matters affecting their work life and welfare. This forces the working public to straddle two different worlds of (1) private employment in nondemocratic decision hierarchies and (2) public citizenship in a robustly democratic political marketplace.

Such a straddle would be most difficult to tolerate for those employed by publicly traded companies whose executives tend to be razor-focused on creating above-average returns for shareholders and less attentive to making their firm more democracy-supporting for their employees. While publicly traded companies make up only 1 percent of US firms, they employ about 33 percent of the US workforce. Due to the canonization of maximizing shareholder value as the only legitimate expression of corporate purpose over the past half century, many managers of publicly listed firms have become increasingly untethered in managing their organizations from the democracy-supporting principles and values that we have been considering in this Element. This helps explains why contemporary political philosophers such as Elizabeth Anderson and Danielle Allen and some organizational economists have become so interested in how these enterprises could play a more explicit democracy-supporting role.[82]

5.1 Pathways to More Democratic Organizations

Such a democracy-supporting role for corporations would need to be premised on the same political equality principle and power-sharing practices we have been discussing. And herein lies the rub. According to traditional thinking about the coordination, control, and management of hierarchical business organizations, people joining such enterprises are expected to give up some degree of

---

[82] See, for example, Elizabeth Anderson, *Private Government*, Princeton University Press, 2017.

personal freedom and voice as part of the employment contract. Job descriptions and titles are on offer, as are wages and various conditions of employment, including benefits. Either one wants to join the enterprise and agrees to the terms of employment, or one does not. After accepting (or negotiating) the terms of employment, most employees have few opportunities and little leverage to shape their work environment. Furthermore, in both publicly owned and privately owned organizations, decision rights over the conduct of the business have long been legally retained by shareholders who invest risk capital in the enterprise and delegate these rights to a board of directors and the firm's senior leadership. For both of these reasons, when joining an established firm, employees cannot expect to play a major role in this decision and control structure unless senior management explicitly invites them to do so.

For democracy-supporting firms, much of this traditional approach to management would need to change so that employees and perhaps other constituencies could participate in corporate deliberations that affect their lives both inside and outside the enterprise. In other words, business policy decisions affecting participants' welfare would need to be discussed, and in some cases shared, with these affected participants – in ways that do not permanently compromise corporate efficiency, competitiveness, and profitability.

This kind of mutual engagement is not, of course, a completely new idea. Several approaches to employee consultation and participation in corporate decision-making have been pursued for decades. Labor unions have forged the longest and most widely recognized approach, which long ago won the right to bargain with company managements on policies and practices affecting the welfare of their employees. Over the years, this right, along with processes for organizing nonunion employees and bargaining with managements on their behalf, has been codified and protected by federal law as both labor and management tested ways to gain advantage in protecting their interests. Another approach known as codetermination was created and mandated as a matter of national economic policy in Germany at the end of World War II and exists to this day. Two other approaches that conceivably can lead to a more democratic consultation and sharing of decision rights within corporations involve employee ownership and Benefit Corporation certification. Both have been pursued voluntarily for years by a small number of managements. However, apart from German-style codetermination, where many business policy decisions are shared with employees through their representatives on companies' supervisory boards, the impact of unionization, employee ownership schemes, and Benefit Corporation certification on the sharing of decision rights has been minimal, both within individual firms and across the economy.

Consider, for example, the case of unionized firms. For the 6 percent of private sector companies that are unionized and employ 11.3 percent of the US workforce (according to the Bureau of Labor Statistics), these employees have indeed gained significant voice in the determination of wages, work rules, length of the workweek, health benefits, and unemployment benefits. However, considering the extremely low and the dramatically declining incidence of unionized companies over the past fifty years, the limited range of negotiable issues under collective bargaining, and the often antagonistic tone of labor–management relations, it is not surprising that few of the negotiating methods and gains associated with unionization have led to collaborative problem-solving beyond the collective bargaining agenda. Most decision and control rights affecting corporate prospects and performance remain firmly in the hands of boards of directors representing shareholders and corporate executives to whom such rights are delegated.

Employee ownership has had limited impact on sharing decision rights within firms, despite some notable pioneers. Employee stock ownership occurs when a company's employees own shares, which can be acquired in a variety of ways. In the United States, the most common route to employee ownership is through an Employee Stock Ownership Plan (ESOP) set up by the company, where employees become the beneficiaries of employer-contributed stock and stock options. Employee Stock Ownership Plans have been around since the mid-1950s, yet employee-owned firms currently represent only a very small portion of the nation's businesses. According to the National Center for Employee Ownership and the US Census Bureau, there are currently 6,257 US companies offering an ESOP versus 6.1 million employer-owned companies. Most of these 6,257 companies are privately held (only 493 are publicly listed), and only a third were 100 percent employee-owned in 2019. While employees in ESOPs appear to be enthusiastic about engaging with management and thrashing out problems together, most do not seem interested in the formal trappings of decision management and control or board representation. Examples of major ESOP companies are Publix Markets (230,000 employees) and W. L. Gore and Associates (maker of Gore-Tex, 12,000 employees). At Publix, employees own about 80 percent of company shares, and the Jenkins family owns the rest. W. L Gore is also a privately held corporation.

Yet another conceivable pathway to more democracy-supporting corporate management is through a firm's voluntary (and time consuming) pursuit of certification as a so-called Benefit Corporation. Benefit Corporations (or B Corps) are not designed explicitly to promote power sharing among corporate stakeholders. However, the value system and management practices of firms that choose to undergo B Corps certification, and then meet the standards B Lab (the nonprofit behind the B Corp certification) sets, are more likely to support new decision-making and power-sharing practices than non-B Corps firms. The mission of certified B Corps is to use business as a force for good. Certification involves committing to nonfinancial impacts of corporate actions and conforming to high standards of accountability and transparency. Many B Corps, for example, pay specific attention to employee benefits and fair employee practices in their supply chains. For example, Patagonia focuses predominantly on its environmental agenda. Adopters of B Corp standards claim that it enables them to pursue a social mission and preserve a collaborative work environment while scaling the business. That said, there are only about 6,000 B Corps in the United States and Canada, including a few large public firms such as Nike and Walmart. But publicly listed B Corps all tend to be closely held by founders or founding families that are able to establish and protect internal governance practices that traditional shareholders might reject. Once again, this population of private and public companies represents a tiny portion of the corporate economy.

Finally, codetermination remains a conceivable route to participating in the decision and control structure of firms. This, however, is not a promising option in the US setting. German-style codetermination involves the legal right of employees to participate in managing the companies they work for through representation on their companies' boards of directors. While codetermination can be seen as a democracy-supporting practice in the workplace, and certainly reflects the egalitarian views of many German (and other non-American) firms, it is in many respects inconsistent with existing state laws governing corporations such as in Delaware, where about 70 percent of Fortune 500 companies and 1.5 million businesses are incorporated. This means that a full-scale adoption of such a legally sanctioned governance structure would require that our current corporate governance model be re-legislated and, inevitably, re-litigated on a state-by-state basis – or somehow superseded by a new federal incorporation statute. This is not easy to implement nor, perhaps, even desirable, in the United States.

In sum, apart from the fallout from the labor union movement, sharing the decision and control rights in the modern corporation through employee ownership and B Corps certification have not been widely impactful, and implementing full codetermination continues to be a serious legal challenge. The low adoption rate of employee ownership and B Corps governance options, plus the substantial legal barriers to integrating codetermination into the US corporate governance regime, leaves us with very weak options for imbuing US corporations with more democracy-supporting features. What's left to be considered is a strategy for changing administrative behavior within the current legal frame-work of American corporate governance in ways that do not freeze decision-making through employee veto or otherwise compromise operating efficiencies. The purpose of such an effort would be to shift traditional command-and-control behavior based on management's unitary decision rights to a management philosophy focused on creating a more "relational environment" with more consultation and selectively shared decision rights among a firm's membership.[83]

What a relational environment means in administrative terms is that business problems affecting the well-being of a firm's members would be solved *with* and *not for* its members. In such an environment, corporate executives and their boards would consider business policies, practices, and strategy for what they often become in practice – namely, agreed-upon outcomes rather than imperial directives. Relational companies understand few matters exist that involve employees and other critical participants in the enterprise where management can realistically expect to hold unitary decision rights, because there are too many interests and blocking behaviors involved. In addition, senior executives operating in a relational environment recognize the legitimacy of a company's key constituencies as discussion and negotiation partners on matters directly affecting their interests.

In relational environments, the great risk is that every business policy becomes negotiable, which would clearly disable firms as an adaptive enterprise in industries undergoing severe cost and technological competition. This can be managed in two ways: first, by promoting the practical idea that inclusiveness and organizational effectiveness are not mutually exclusive; and second, by thinking through the mix of issues that sensibly fall into the "discussible" and "negotiable" categories and those that do not. The precise mix of issues qualifying for joint discussion, negotiation, and power sharing will vary from company to company depending on their idiosyncratic operating circumstances and the constituency interests. The mix of qualifying matters could be trad-itional labor-management issues such as working conditions and wages, health and safety, reorganizations, plant openings and closings, employee transfers and reductions, and the introduction of new technologies affecting working condi-tions and job security. In most relational companies, matters related to corporate financing and financial structure, dividend policy, changes in ownership (M&A transactions), and R&D investment might be discussed with employees for informational purposes only. For active investors and creditors, however, these matters have always been, and would certainly remain, fair game for

---

[83] "Relational environment" is Danielle Allen's phrase, *Justice by Means of Democracy*, p. 172.

direct negotiation, especially where threats of corporate takeover and the management replacement are concerned.

The United States has a long history of providing both occasional and permanent interactive forums where such matters can be addressed – forums where information can be shared, joint problem-solving can take root, and power sharing can eventually become a recognized and validated pathway to finding practical solutions to constituency conflicts. Such forums have existed, and exist today, under many names and titles: labor–management committees at local and corporate levels, joint study committees and employee engagement committees, continuous improvement councils, quarterly town hall meetings, and face-to-face meetings with top-level executives. Each of these forums helps keep employees (and other key constituencies) engaged with their companies, gives employees an opportunity to influence working conditions and practices, improves work relationships, increases both team and operational effectiveness, bolsters job satisfaction, and fully engages employees in the life of the enterprise. Additional benefits of such problem-solving and power-sharing forums include their role in creating truly cooperative organizations with low coordination costs based on reciprocal relationships – rather than disunited organizations generating unnecessarily high costs of coordinating parties with conflicting interests and agendas.

As we have seen, public ownership of companies can complicate the implementation of such a management refocus, but that does not invalidate or repudiate relationality, power sharing or, as I discuss next, the principle of reciprocity that motivates effective power sharing.

5.2 Reciprocity and Power Sharing

If reciprocity is to be the democracy-supporting principle that underlies and legitimizes power sharing in hierarchical profit-seeking enterprises, what, precisely, does reciprocity call for?

Reciprocity, writes Danielle Allen, is at the heart of justice.[84] Adopting the habit of reciprocity enables the possibility that interacting parties – whether they be friends, fellow citizens, business partners, or employees – can achieve some form of "egalitarian engagement" in solving problems that affect their lives.

The reciprocity principle has a long and distinguished history, starting with Aristotle, who wrote that the concept refers to an exemplary kind of social cooperation, where transacting parties preserve parity in utility of benefits

---

[84] Allen, *Justice by Means of Democracy*, p. 42.

exchanged over time.[85] To meet the (ethical) standard of reciprocity, the utility value of goods and skills exchanged must be proportional to each party's perceived needs and wants.[86] If one party gets richer at the other's expense, reciprocity does not exist. Indeed, one party has more than one's due share and the other suffers the injustice of having less. Similarly, the value of each party's needs and wants can only be accurately and fairly established if relevant exchange negotiations are free from the domination of one party over another. Where there is no voluntary exchange, there is no reciprocity and, thus, no power sharing (only power hoarding).

Important about reciprocal exchanges is that they are the result of a bargain struck between parties setting their own terms of exchange.[87] The parties estimate their own want satisfactions that they will derive from the goods or skills they will get in exchange for their own goods or skills. In subsequent bargaining, parties arrive at an exchange ratio that is an intermediate or mutually determined ratio between the two (pre-bargaining) estimations of want satisfactions. In the absence of domination of one party over another, this exchange ratio establishes each transacting party's "reserve price" for cooperation. And because the context of exchange relationships in business continually change, reciprocity is best understood as a procedural matter, based on dialogue and periodic revisits of prior agreements, where new agreements or contracts can be forged, and reimbursements or other paybacks can take place if one party has been disadvantaged in the past.

When the reserve price of all parties is met through the exchange of quid pro quos and, often, mutual sacrifice of short-term personal gains for long-term, shared benefits, the moral integrity of the exchange remains intact. Such exchanges are also tangible expressions of reciprocity and power sharing that democratic capitalism needs in order to keep its moral legitimacy undivided.

In corporations where the principle of reciprocity is adopted as a behavioral guideline and a moral constraint on shareholder wealth maximization,

---

[85] Danielle S. Allen, *Talking to Strangers*, University of Chicago Press, 2004, p. 131. Aristotle refers to this as an "exchange of equivalents."

[86] Josef Soudek, "Aristotle's Theory of Exchange: An Inquiry into the Origin of Economic Analysis," *Proceedings of the American Philosophical Society*, 96, no. 1, February 1952, pp. 45–75. Throughout the discussion of the reciprocity principle, I have relied heavily upon Soudek's analysis of Aristotle's theory of exchange and the relevance of reciprocal justice principles to economics and management.

[87] As Soudek points out (p. 64), money serves as a useful medium for expressing wants and thus the value of goods and services exchanged, and greatly facilitates exchange by transforming subjective, qualitative phenomena like wants and want satisfactions into objective, quantitative ones.

shareholders (as the residual bearers of risk in all incorporated enterprises) continue to hold a preeminent position in the hierarchy of corporate stakeholders with expectations of a return on their investment sufficient to compensate them for the uncontrollable and often unknowable risks they bear. This expected return is, of course, shareholders' reserve price (or required rate of return) for investing risk capital in the enterprise. But shareholders are not the only party with a reserve price for participating in the organization's work. Other parties – such as employees, suppliers, customers, creditors, neighbors, and guardians of the environment – also have their reserve prices, too, related in part to the risks that they bear through their voluntary (and sometimes involuntary) participation in the life of the enterprise. In the absence of total domination by capital, their participation in and support for the enterprise depends on a surplus of benefits for their continued collaboration or, at the very least, a level of valued benefits above an imagined breakeven exchange.

In the world of business (and politics), reciprocity is difficult to sustain despite best intentions. This is because reciprocity always requires, as suggested, a certain amount of personal or institutional sacrifice.[88] Sacrifice – namely, the surrender of something valued or desired for the sake of something regarded as having a higher or more pressing claim – is as central to the world of business as it is to the practice of democracy and democratic citizenship. With respect to democracy, for example, sacrifice involves accepting defeat after a hard-fought election. In this way, sacrifice builds community (and discourages violence). Sacrifice in the world of business involves a willingness to defer (surrender) corporate and personal gains to maintain the long-term health of the enterprise and the economic system. This, we shall see, is where experiments with reciprocal management meet their greatest challenge. Sacrifice involves tolerating a certain amount of disappointment and psychological pain, which often triggers nonrational, systematic behaviors that are intimately linked with the brain's fight-or-flight responses. Economist Michael Jensen refers to this behavior as "pain avoidance," a nonrational but fixed behavior that tends to block change of all kinds, including the kind of corporate governance changes we are discussing here.[89] Although the phenomenon of pain avoidance as a barrier to change deserves more discussion than I can afford here, it is, in my experience, an ever-present barrier to our willingness to suffer a short-term loss to gain a long-term benefit (such as a democracy-supporting ideal).

---

[88] Allen, *Talking to Strangers*, p. 37ff.

[89] Michael C. Jensen, "Self-Interest, Altruism, Incentives, and Agency Theory," *Journal of Applied Corporate Finance*, 7, no. 2, Summer 1994, pp. 40–45.

5.3 Examples of Reciprocity and Power Sharing in Practice

So, with this warning, what evidence do we have about how reciprocity and power sharing can and do work in practice? One source is companies founded and led by activist-minded entrepreneurs who willingly pursued reciprocity in creating relational work environments as an expression of their own (democratic) belief systems and theories of management. Companies in this category include the previously mentioned Publix Markets, W. L Gore & Associates, and Patagonia, each of which has a public record of continuity and estimable commercial success. Significantly, the shares of these companies – all controlled by founding families – are not publicly traded, and the CEOs have unfettered freedom to manage things the way they desire.

In the US setting, publicly listed companies that have attempted to create relational work environments (often by becoming employee-owned) typically have been forced to do so by dire competitive and financial factors. When this pressure subsides, or when outside entities takeover the companies, a reversion in the direction of prior, nonrelational governance practices often sets in as the financial and competitive context changes. Perhaps the classic example of the disappearing revolution in corporate governance is Weirton Steel Corporation, formerly one of the world's largest producers of tin plate products. In the 1980s, Weirton Steel became the largest employee-owned steel plant in the world when the company offered employees stock ownership as a way to negotiate concessions with unions to avoid bankruptcy. After 2004, when the company declared bankruptcy and eventually disappeared into the portfolio of a Luxembourg multinational steel manufacturing corporation, the employee ownership and power-sharing revolution at Weirton Steel likewise vanished.

A less well-known case, but one more profound in the scope and scale of governance changes attempted, involves General Motors Corporation.[90] In 1981, at the peak of the Japanese small-car onslaught, GM was forced to scrap its plans for an American-made small car – the S-car – to take on the imports. After years of publicly denying the existence of a Japanese competitive advantage, GM, through its own internal analyses of the cost to produce the proposed S-car, confirmed that such a car simply could not compete on a manufacturing cost basis. At the end of 1983, a GM–UAW Joint Study Center was announced to rethink how to build a small car. After three short weeks, the ninety-nine-member committee had developed a "statement of philosophy" that reflected the kind of management–labor relationship they believed was necessary for GM to compete. Note that this statement was not

---

[90] See David Dyer, Malcolm S. Salter, and Alan M. Webber, *Changing Alliances*, Harvard Business School Press, 1987.

about workplace democracy per se, but rather about institutional survival, job security, and company values. The statement of the Study Committee read, in part:

> We believe that all people want to be involved in decisions that affect them, care about their jobs, take pride in themselves and in their contributions, and want to share in the success of their efforts.
>
> By creating an atmosphere of mutual trust and respect, recognizing and utilizing individual expertise and knowledge in innovative ways, providing the technologies and education for each individual, we will enjoy a successful relationship and a sense of belonging to an integrated business system capable of achieving our common goals, which ensures security for our people and success for our business and communities.

The study's participants explained how this philosophy could help GM meet its goal of reducing costs and improving quality. For example, trust between management and labor would reduce the need for management layers and supervision (overhead). This philosophy also served as a template for testing the design of the S-car manufacturing subsystems, including plant layout and design, technology, work units, and job design. The tangible result of all this collaborative work was GM's decision in January 1985 to go forward with its "clean sheet" approach to building a competitive small car in the United States under the Saturn nameplate. Saturn would not only be a separate brand (the first new one added since 1918) but also a separate (wholly owned) corporation with endowed assets of $5 billion.

Many of the principles the Joint Study Committee expressed and embedded in the Saturn Corporation were further codified in the corporate-wide 1984 labor contract between GM and the UAW. A variety of joint GM–UAW committees were created to carry out different elements of the contract agreement, to share information, to discuss common problems, and to develop a shared perspective. The introduction of Saturn-like joint committees was designed to change the long-embedded, noncooperative, entirely transactional mode of interaction between management and union employees. Historically, plant managers had cracked the whip; they had ensured that discipline and control were maintained on the shop floor (but the discipline was bad, including absenteeism, drinking alcohol on the production line, and petty acts of product sabotage such as putting Coke bottles inside door panels that would rattle and annoy customers). And the local union president had responded in kind. They won elections by showing that they could and would stand up to the boss by filing waves of grievances or refusing to go along with changes that threatened to boost productivity. The new committee structure promised to alleviate this situation. Rather than making the plant manager and local president less important, the committees made them vital elements in establishing the new management–employee relationship, where their joint-decision-making (power sharing) became the building block of competitiveness.

Under the philosophy so painstakingly worked out and nurtured at Saturn, small groups of workers were given wide latitude to participate in developing company policy, even to the point of reviewing the company's annual plan; teams of workers created job descriptions of group and team leaders, instead of the other way around; and hourly workers participated in developing their own work. Workers were accorded job security, authority, and responsibility for their own operations, as well as equal respect and status with management (no distinctions between the two sides in either the parking lot or the cafeteria). In brief, the same set of behaviors and quid pro quos negotiated between management and labor in Japan were present.

The creation of Saturn Corporation, together with the 1984 labor contract, illustrates that GM's dire competitive fight for survival was sufficient to force the kind reciprocity (job security for changes in work rules) and power sharing (joint committees). Initially, external objective measurements rewarded these efforts, which demonstrate that both the need for change and the direction of change were well considered (and in line with democracy-supporting). Throughout the 1980s, GM recorded significant improvements in product quality and productivity, as well as plant-level factors such as absenteeism, grievances, and unauthorized work stoppages – all of which provided workers with the greatest possibilities for job security. This slice of GM–UAW history shows that a relational environment can be created in designated facilities in large public corporations when the economic incentives are sufficient. GM's history also shows, however, that sustaining and spreading this relational environment beyond the newly cocreated facilities at Saturn Corporation was not ultimately successful due to decades of management intransigence and sour labor relations throughout the greater GM production system.

There is of course much, much more to GM's story. In the case of the Saturn Corporation, despite early success in the 1990s (Saturn was the third best-selling car model in the United States in 1994), the venture ultimately failed because senior GM executives outside of the Saturn Corporation subsidiary could not see the benefits of new ways of doing things and a new kind of organizational culture! GM insisted on managing all of its automotive divisions centrally, and the leadership at both GM and the UAW demanded that Saturn get in line with traditional ways of doing things. GM wanted Saturn to be like the rest of its offerings, a compilation of standard GM parts with a different nameplate, not a different kind of car manufactured and sold in a different way. Corporate executives lectured Saturn that the GM corporate way was more profitable, because it used the same parts across many automobile platforms. Saturn cars (and their marketing) soon became more generic and lost their differentiated consumer appeal. As for the UAW, Local 1810 at Saturn also came under constant fire from above to get in line. One local president was removed from his position by the UAW, and a successor was treated as a heretic for wanting, as he put it, to "create a viable model for the labor union in our modern era." Saturn people, he believed, didn't think of themselves as GM subordinates or as UAW card carriers. They were Saturn team members with a common mission. And for that, team leaders and members were ostracized and criticized. By 2009, a year after the great financial crisis, GM found itself in serious financial trouble once again as demand evaporated and it was forced to file for a Chapter 11 bankruptcy reorganization and seek a government bailout. In the end, GM was unsuccessful in exporting the plant's relational environment and lean production to the rest of its US operations.

GM and the US auto industry were not alone in the 1980s (and before) to experiment with nonadversarial worker–management collaborative committees addressing specific issues related to the quality of work, cost savings, job restructuring, safety, training, and the quality of work–life in general. Before the Saturn experiment, there were thousands of joint management–employee committees established at the plant level during World War II to increase wartime production. (Many disappeared after the war.) During the economic adjustments of the 1980s, economic circumstances forced the textile, clothing, semiconductor, telecommunications, and health care industries to forge more cooperative and less shareholder-value-maximizing labor–management relations. There is also a long history of industry-level committees or forums with management and employee representatives working at the national level in the ladies garment industry, the construction industry, and the textile manufacturing industry, including such companies as DuPont, Burlington Mills, and J.P. Stevens. Finally, we have a rich history of geographic area committees or forums established to improve the job climate and attract new business enterprises, as well national, multi-party forums, some entirely private, focused on enhanced productivity and matters of economic policy, health care policy, and various issues of common concern. Today, that history continues. The health care company KaiserPermanente has nearly 4,000 teams of management and labor representatives coming together to joint problem-solve about company operations and to give employees a direct voice in their work.[91] Ford Motor Company and many others instituted employee engagement and continuous

---

[91] Roy E. Bahat, Thomas A. Kochan, and Liba Wenig Rubenstein, "The Labor Savvy Leader," *Harvard Business Review*, July–August 2023, p. 74.

improvement teams at the plant level. Levi Strauss is well-known for its efforts to build a more equitable and inclusive organization with DEI (diversity, equity, and inclusion) teams spread throughout the company. And in the fall of 2023 as the impact of artificial intelligence (AI) on the future of work and employment levels emerged in industries as disparate as Hollywood script writers and auto workers, calls were being made by one of the nation's leading labor experts to consider legislation requiring companies to set up employee advisory boards (power-sharing forums) to give workers some say in how AI would be deployed.[92] It is unclear how, in the absence of such legislated forums, nonunion workers could influence the policy affecting their livelihoods. The good news, however, is that we have a long and continuing history of firms experimenting with relational engagement and other elements of democracy-supporting management practices upon which we can build.

The less good news involves the status of federal labor law. Today, many of the collaborative committees or forums cited earlier are only allowed under the National Labor Relations Act (1935) in companies that are unionized. The Act *prohibits* nonunion employer–worker collaborations out of fear of management domination of these committees. As a result, employee voice and information flows from employees are severely compromised in nonunion settings. Forums for cooperation and reciprocity are now being shut down, precisely when new avenues to worker voice and participation are most needed. What's clearly required is amending section 8(a)(2) of the National Labor Relations Act (NLRA), which prohibits the creation of nonunion worker–management committees. To prevent management from controlling or manipulating such forums, advocates (such as American Compass, best known for its work in building a new conservative economic agenda) have suggested that workers must support their creation through a free and fair election and must have the power to dissolve it by withdrawing that consent. In 2022, Republican Senator Marco Rubio and Congressman Jim Banks introduced legislation to this effect. This legislation deserves broad support.

5.4 Commonalities in Firms Practicing Reciprocity and Power Sharing

One clear commonality across firms seeking to develop more relational environments is the motivating fear of catastrophic economic breakdown. The possibility of a financial collapse has been a huge incentive to restructure (and

---

[92] See comments of Thomas Kochan, professor at the MIT School of Management, quoted by Hiawatha Bray in, "Hollywood Writers Won Their AI Battle: What about the Rest of Us?" *The Boston Globe*, September 30, 2023, p. D1.

renegotiate) long-standing relations with industrial partners throughout the industrial hierarchy. It remains to be seen if the call to renovate democratic capitalism offers a sufficient incentive to foster the kind of power sharing discussed throughout this Element in the absence of an economic crisis.

Another commonality is that when entrepreneurial companies such as Body Shop, Aveda, Tom's of Maine, and Whole Foods – all created with a social, environmental, or relational agenda – are acquired by large public corporations such as L'Oreal, Estee Lauder, Colgate Palmolive, and Amazon, the companies' founding agenda often faces financial pressures to focus on growing revenues and earnings for shareholders.[93] The same is true for private companies becoming publicly listed and inviting outside capital that seeks above-average returns into the enterprise.

A further commonality is the fact that virtually no agreements between management, employees, and other parties could have been reached unless each participant in the negotiating or power-sharing forum was prepared to give something to others – involving a mutual sacrifice or surrendering of interests and rights. For company managers, power sharing has meant accepting an irrevocable commitment to share some aspects of strategy making and implementation with other industrial actors. As noted, power sharing differs from yielding decision-making, but it does require enormous skill and patience in shaping the content of the discussion and identifying the trade-offs to be made when considering the various interests at stake.

We should not be under the illusion that redefining the nature of corporate stewardship in this way is an easy task. It requires strong commitment and moral leadership on the part of corporate management and boards of directors to take on such a role when working under unrelating shareholder demands for increased profitability. This raises questions such as the following: What kind of moral culture is needed to encourage and reinforce such leadership in our political economy? How can we best advance a moral culture where business and political leaders are less self-interested and more concerned with the perceived legitimacy of democratic capitalism and the illuminating ideal it offers the nation going forward?

6 A Moral Culture for Democratic Capitalism

In his 1796 farewell address, after six years as commander-in-chief of the Continental Army and another eight years as president of the United States, George Washington warned the states that a national morality is

---

[93] See Geoffrey Jones, *Deeply Responsible Business: A Global History of Value-Driven Leadership*, Harvard University Press, 2023.

paramount in supporting the American system – that moral requirements were needed to sustain the republican form of government that the Founders had envisioned. He said: "Of all the disposition and habits which lead to political prosperity ... morality is a necessary spring of popular government." Today, 228 years later, we must ask ourselves whether Washington's exhortation about the need for a national morality is a realistic expectation. Is it possible today to have a widely shared moral culture supportive of democratic capitalism in a nation that includes wide variances in demographics and philosophical predispositions? If so, how would we define such a culture? And how could we best advance a vision of a country that is less self-interested, more mutual, and more in line with true democratic capitalism?

6.1 Relevant Norms and Values

Culture is defined by a set of social norms and values that guide behavior. Families often develop (largely idiosyncratic) cultures of their own. So, too, do business firms and political economies – in response to a mix of historical factors.[94] Take, for example, the culture of corporate America, which refers to the population of large firms that play such a dominant role in our political economy. Economics writer David Leonhardt has opined that in the decades following the great economic crisis known as the Great Depression, "the prevailing culture of corporate America called for restraining self-interest in the name of national interest."[95] The self-interest Leonhardt referred to involved easing back from short-term profit maximization. National interest involved recovering from the widely shared economic pain of the 1930s. This contemporary culture, according to Leonhardt, "explains why corporate executives helped build a high-wage economy and accepted high taxes on their incomes. They were willing to sacrifice their own short-term interests for what they considered to be larger causes, including political stability and American power."[96]

Note that Leonhardt's characterization of the post-Depression corporate culture makes no reference to society's laws or governing institutions pertaining to sacrifice. That's because culture is distinct from the law, even though law and culture influence each other greatly. Here is Leonhardt's simple but evocative observation:

---

[94] See Joel Mokyr, *A Culture of Growth: The Origins of the Modern Economy*, Princeton University Press, 2016, p. 8 for a discussion of culture in an economic and political context.

[95] David Leonhardt, *Ours Was the Shining Future*, Random House, 2023, p. 261.

[96] Ibid., p. 262.

Institutions and laws tend to revolve around rules that dictate how people must behave. Culture involves more judgement. The law says that a customer must pay a restaurant bill and that an employer must pay at least minimum wage. Culture affects how much of a tip the customer leaves and how much more than minimum wage an employer pays an entry-level worker.[97]

For the most part, Leonhardt is perfectly correct: culture involves extralegal values and standards.

The norms and values defining national culture, industry culture, or corporate culture can be moral or not. The standards against which these norms and values can be judged to be moral and responsible commonly include honesty, trustworthiness, and lawfulness. All certainly support democratic capitalism.[98] But, as I have argued throughout this Element, an important addition to any such list of moral values needs to be a deep commitment to both political equality and reciprocity as key enablers. Without political equality and reciprocity as core values, there cannot be a true democracy. And without a true democracy, there can be no true democratic capitalism.

In the words of philosopher and democracy theorist Danielle Allen, "the realization of democracy as a political form depends upon maximizing the trajectory toward *political equality*."[99] To this important thought, I add the idea that if the realization of democracy depends on political equality as a core value and reciprocity as one of its most important facets, then it stands to reason that the perceived legitimacy of democratic capitalism also depends on including political equality in the mix of values that define the moral culture of true democratic capitalism.

Embedding political equality and reciprocity as core values in a political economy long dominated by self-interest and personal utility maximization is not an easy task. On the business side of our political economy, we have seen that the values of political equality and reciprocity that developed between a group of GM executives and UAW employees during their competitive and financial crisis of the 1980s and 1990s, was, in the end, an isolated response to an existential threat mounted by Japanese automakers. Once competitive conditions in the US auto industry appeared to ease, the never-before-seen practices of reciprocity and power sharing at the creation of the Saturn Corporation receded as GM and UAW leaders fell back on the traditional management–labor relations model, where the name of the game was maximizing economic

---

[97] Ibid., p. 51.

[98] See Michael Novak, "Democratic Capitalism," *National Review*, September 24, 2013, for a discussion of moral and cultural practices consistent with democratic capitalism and "the prospering of free societies."

[99] Allen, *Justice by Means of Democracy*, p. 35.

self-interest and negotiating leverage. A corporate culture embodying political equality and reciprocity turned out not to be a "sticky" feature of capitalism.

On the political side of our political economy, we have seen similar passing moments of reciprocity and cooperation in the aftermath of the subprime mortgage banking crisis of 2008 (when members of Congress came together to authorize $800 billion to stabilize the US financial market and promote economic recovery), and the COVID-19 pandemic (when Congress came together in March 2021 to pass the historic American Rescue Plan that made investments to crush the virus, create millions of jobs, provide direct relief to working families, and help schools open safely). But once these crises passed, political conduct reverted to normal contentiousness, which in the intervening years has come to define our increasingly polarized and fractious democracy. Political equality and reciprocity turn out not to be a "sticky" feature of democracy either.

All this may seem perfectly normal. But the deeply troubling question for those of us concerned about the future of democratic capitalism as a credible governance ideal is whether sufficient incentives exist for American society to shift our governance culture further in the direction of political equality, reciprocity, and more relational norms.

From my perspective, the answer to this question is "not without a great deal of public education regarding the national stakes involved and credible leadership that brings public attention to the existential risks that we are running." Currently, there is little or no push by our business leaders, political candidates, or elected officials to coalesce around a new or expanded set of democracy-supporting norms and values. The only exception to this pattern is the rising number of public-spirited, bipartisan, democracy reform advocates like Partners in Democracy, Equal Citizens, and Issue One beginning to spring up across the country.

Perhaps some unexpected economic or political crisis, or external threat, will change the general public's state of mind and deepen fears about our future as a true democracy. But barring catastrophe, I see little evidence that the nation broadly believes we have now reached such a tipping point or that we need to start questioning whether our social norms and values are still true or workable and whether a different kind of conduct or set of relationships might make more sense.[100]

Consistent with this apparent lack of a popular push to embed the moral principles of political equality and reciprocity more deeply into our business

---

[100] For an important discussion about the triggers of cultural change, see Ann Swindler, "Culture in Action: Symbols and Strategies," *American Sociological Review*, 51, no. 2, April 1986, pp. 273–286. Referenced in Leonhardt's discussion of how culture changes over time, p. 51.

and political culture are the powerful incentives that discourage the development of more relational and democracy-supporting values. Stories about cronyism and restricted suffrage make this point clear.

In the cronyism story, the incentives that drive corporate executives and other wealthy elites to collude with the political class for their private benefit (in seeking a favorable regulatory environment, government subsidies, tax breaks, and intentionally ambiguous laws that can be easily gamed) are huge. At the top of the list, these incentives include the preservation and enhancement of their privileged position as society's most powerful and rationally self-interested participants. For society's economic and political elites, the disincentives to change behavior and an enabling culture are massive.

In the restricted suffrage story, huge incentives are at work counteracting the democratization of the right to vote and the right to run for political office. As previously discussed, parties in control of state legislatures and Congressional representatives, along with incumbents, have great personal incentives to protect their incumbency and extend their tenure in the political arena through election practices that restrict ballot access, curtail the influx of newcomers to political office, and limit the menu of candidate choices.

Despite the currently high institutional barriers to change in the values that define our current economic and political culture, we all know that the need to change often exists before it becomes obvious. That's where we are today. The need to change the norms and values driving our current system of economic and political governance is expressed in aforementioned surveys reporting a radical decline of public trust and confidence in both democracy and capitalism (and the governance of our political economy) among many demographic groups.

These survey results should not surprise us. When a national culture like ours celebrates, let alone tolerates, narrowly defined concepts of self-interest and self-preservation, it naturally puts civic society at risk driving the polity into rivalrous, noncooperating groups. This is what we are experiencing today as our business and political communities become increasingly oriented toward claiming as much advantage for the self and ignoring the well-being and representation of others as part of one's own self-interest. Crony capitalism is a prime example of this phenomenon, as are the increasing restrictions on universal suffrage being established by highly partisan and self-interested elected officials and their political parties through gerrymandering, ballot access restrictions, and revised voting procedures. Under these conditions, finding common purposes and policies, let alone a sense of justice, is nigh on impossible.

Our great challenge, then, is to perfect ways of nudging our national culture in a direction that is less rooted in self-interest and more aligned with community and national interests, as George Washington exhorted the nation in 1796.

Such a cultural shift is unlikely to take place on its own without a broad social mandate or effective evangelical effort. In the absence of such a mandate, it is unreasonable to expect that current economic and political actors will voluntarily ignore long-embedded incentives that reward the pursuit of narrowly defined self-interest – whether they be highly paid corporate executives whose total compensation is tightly linked to their companies' share price or elected officials who stand to gain from uncontested elections.

This leaves the singular option of relying on unrelenting persuasion of the kind that could help our business and political communities rethink what norms and values could best guide our unique form of democratic capitalism going forward. The history of successful economic and political movements in our country and elsewhere shows that to be effective, such persuasion needs to be rooted in compelling research and writings of movement leaders or spokespersons, education at local levels throughout the country, and respected evangelists in the business and political communities speaking out in support of, in this case, a renewed democratic capitalism.

The first step in mounting such a culture campaign is alerting the public to the dangers to truly *democratic* capitalism posed by the kind of excessive self-interest and personal utility maximization that drives today's pervasive cronyism and restricted suffrage. Perhaps such a wakeup call could feature publicizing the social costs of what years of polling data documents as a nosedive in citizen trust and confidence in both capitalism and democracy. Beyond that, however, such a campaign will require, from the very beginning, an appeal to a higher loyalty than the maximization of personal self-interest. That higher loyalty needs to be far more consistent with the democratic element of democratic capitalism than narrow conceptions of self-interest or the maximization of personal utility.

6.2 Committing to Fairness and Reciprocity

What might that higher loyalty be? What shared social value or idea is *more* important to the future of democratic capitalism as a governance system than our current, dogged pursuit of individual utility maximization?

There are at least two answers to this question. One answer, which does not reach for an explicit moral or ethical justification, involves simply committing to a broader conception of self-interest than individual utility maximization in day-to-day decision-making – for practical reasons. For example, business school professors like Bower, Leonard, and Paine describe in their study of capitalism at risk how forward-thinking companies "recognize that their health and prosperity are deeply intertwined with the health and prosperity of the market system as a whole" and voluntarily adopt "strategies and behaviors that help reinforce and strengthen the system" – thereby serving their long-term business interests while at the same time "performing a civic responsibility."[101] Referencing the French political thinker Alexis de Tocqueville, they refer to this broader conception of corporate self-interest, which includes the interests of others with whom they interact on a continuing basis, as "self-interest properly understood." This, of course, is eminently sensible from an economic point of view.

A second answer relies more directly on moral principle. Because we are discussing the renovation of democratic capitalism as a system of economic and political governance, I suggest Aristotle's principle of justice, which is best understood as "fairness in the process of governing," as the most appropriate moral principle. This justice principle is a good place to anchor a moral culture that supports democratic capitalism because it recognizes the need to provide voice and influence for all members of the national community in formulating business and public policies that affect their well-being. No other principle or value comes closer to the essence of democracy than this.

Adopting the Aristotelian notion of fairness as a cornerstone of a moral culture supportive of democratic capitalism requires careful attention to what, precisely, makes the democracy component of our governance system "fair." I have argued throughout this Element that political equality and, especially, its all-important facet of reciprocity are the critical enabling conditions for fairness in a democratic state.

To recall our earlier discussion, reciprocity refers to an exemplary kind of social cooperation in a transactional setting. Reciprocity, if nothing else, is a relational concept focused on mutuality – not an individualistic concept focused on the maximization and preservation of self-interest.

Aristotle argued that for the economic basis of society to be both secure and ethical, every exchange in economic markets, and by implication political markets, must be an exchange of equivalent value. In other words, market exchanges cannot be sustained unless the exchange partners are assured that what they give away and what they receive are of equivalent value to them. For this to happen, some principle or shared value is required to hold people

---

[101] Joseph L. Bower, Herman B. Leonard, and Lynn S. Paine, *Capitalism at Risk*, Harvard Business Review Press, 2011, p. 150.

together. That principle is what Aristotle defines as "reciprocal justice" or reciprocity, which involves equivalent or proportional returns between contracting parties. To meet the standard of reciprocal justice, the utility value of the items exchanged must be equal (actually, proportional) to each party's perceived needs and wants. If one party gets richer at the other's expense in this exchange, reciprocal justice would not be realized – because one party would receive a supernormal award and the other would suffer the injustice of having less. This supports a point I made earlier in this Element – this exchange can only be considered fair and just if the negotiations between the parties are free from the domination of one party over the other.[102] Relatedly, it is only when the reserve price of all parties is met through the exchange of quid pro quos free from domination that the moral integrity of the exchange remains intact. For business readers, nothing in this definition of fairness and reciprocity requires investors or other suppliers of capital to take a discount from their risk-adjusted required rate of return (their reserve price), unless such a cut leads to compensating returns in future time periods.

Aristotle's principles of fairness and reciprocity provide the essential organizing ideas for all democratic regimes (such as democratic capitalism) – namely, the idea that democratic societies are basically fair systems of social cooperation among free and equal persons.[103] Social cooperation in this context includes the idea of "fair terms of cooperation," implying notions of reciprocity or mutuality that I have touted throughout this Element as guiding principles for the restoration of democratic capitalism. (The "toxic duo" of cronyism and restricted voice are two democracy-destroying examples of the lack of fairness and reciprocity.)

Of course, fairness and reciprocity do not stand alone as the only moral principles relevant to the renovation of American democracy. But they need to command a leading position. Consider, for example, the important moral principle of freedom. While fairness is about ensuring that everyone is treated in a politically equal way, freedom is a matter of personal liberty and the ability to live one's life as one sees fit. Freedom is certainly a core moral principle embedded in our national ideology ("liberty and justice for all" in our Pledge of Alliance), and its intellectual provenance in the world of political economy is certainly a distinguished one. Some refer to freedom as "America's national creed."[104] But it is arguable that freedom cannot be sustained independently

---

[102] Again, see Soudek, "Aristotle's Theory of Exchange," pp. 45–75.

[103] John Rawls, *Justice as Fairness: A Restatement*, The Belknap Press of Harvard University Press, 2001.

[104] Leonhardt, *Ours Was the Shining Future*, p. 377. In the name of freedom came the American revolution, abolition of slavery, trust-busting, women's suffrage, the rise of organized labor, civil rights laws, same sex marriages, and so on.

from Aristotle's principle of justice as fairness. This is because, in the absence of justice or fairness, the weak would easily be dominated over time by the strong, both economically and politically, and only the powerful would end up possessing freedom.[105] This is the lesson that today's pervasive cronyism in our political economy teaches us.

6.3 Socializing Moral Values

If we accept fairness and reciprocity as our higher loyalty, then the question becomes how to socialize and build commitment to these governance principles and their underlying values more broadly than we have been able to do in recent decades. There are several ways of doing so: by *proclamation*, where norms, values, and preferences are spread via autocratic fiat and enforced by state power, such as under the Third Reich; by *revolution*, where values are reprioritized via popular uprising and the power of the polis, as in the American and French revolutions and in various revolutionary theocratic republics today; by *legislation*, where values are legitimized, diffused, and enforced via democratic legislative action and legal compliance, such as in the United States with civil rights, social security, health care, voting rights, and competition policy; and by *moral suasion* via evangelism and social movements.

None of these categories are totally discrete. There is certainly overlap among them (as between moral suasion as a precursor to legislation), yet they do suggest a conceptually differentiated set of activities based on the source of power driving changes in social norms, values, and preferences. Much can be said about each way of socializing norms and values, which is beyond the scope of this Element – other than to say we need to focus on *moral suasion* as the most promising and relevant route to renovating democratic capitalism. Socialization of moral values via proclamation requires the police power of the state to implement, which is totally unacceptable (unimaginable) in the US context and, in any case, a sign of the kind of moral degradation we are trying to avoid. Revolution, apart from its incalculable social costs, is not called for in our current economic and political circumstance. Legislation, unless nested in a strong compliance culture and broadly united polis, inevitably leads to the gaming of rule-writing in Congress, more run-arounds of new rules in pursuing economic and political self-interest, and other ways of corrupting democratic governance such as through pervasive cronyism.

---

[105] See David Gordon, "Freedom vs. Justice: Are They in Conflict?" Mises Wire (Mises Institute), March 10, 2016. For a full discussion. https://mises.org/library/freedom-vs-justice-are-they-conflict.

Moral suasion, especially through social movements, however, offers a different path to changed cultural values and norms. Deva Woodly's highly relevant work on social movements demonstrates the capacity to change "canonical thinking" and modify our understanding of politics and the range of political and cultural possibilities open to us. She writes: "Social movements infuse the essential elements of pragmatic imagination, social intelligence, and democratic experimentation into public spheres that are ailing and have become nonresponsive, stagnant, and/or closed."[106] Her most recent account of the Movement for Black Lives Matter (M4BL) that emerged in 2014 – along with the differentiated histories of the Tea Party movement starting in 2009, the Occupy movement in 2011, and the #Me Too movement in 2017 – shows how social movements can catch fire in multiple ways depending on the local social landscape, political context, ecology of existing citizen-action groups, and choice of leadership structure.

According to Woodly, social movements comprise a way of meeting, engaging, educating, and preparing for collective action to serve some public cause. Social movements present in a wide variety of forms, with two iconic forms anchoring the ends of a full spectrum of possibilities and representing two vastly different approaches to leadership and followership. The first takes its energy and direction from a dominant leader and leadership group that seeds local chapters or associations and provides programmatic and political support. This type builds power and influence through publicly known advocates and proselytizers with concrete ideas for a possible future in mind. The development and remarkable success of the Committee for Economic Development (CED) described later in this section is a good example of this type of social movement.

The second iconic type of social movement is more organic and widely distributed in society, comprised of existing, community-based organizations with shared interests that choose to coordinate activities and seek shared goals in response to a crisis or overwhelming moment affecting society at large. This social movement model notably does not include a single didactic leader, yet it is richly "leaderful" – meaning that the movement has multiple leaders and a diffuse leadership with little coordination by a national body.[107] The Movement for Black Lives Woodly described is an archetypical example of this type of social movement – one that was in place before the killing of George Floyd in May 2020 nationalized the agenda of M4BL.

The main challenge of relying on moral suasion and social movement organizing as a means of socializing new norms and values is that it requires

---

[106] Deva R. Woodly, *Reckoning: Black Lives Matter and the Democratic Necessity of Social Movements*, Oxford University Press, 2022, pp. xi, xvi, 4, and 17.

[107] Ibid., p. 44.

a long-term, sustained effort with uncertain returns. Still, abundant evidence exists that such strategies for changing cultural and political values need not end up as a fool's errand.

In the specific realm of the political economy, David Leonhardt provides a good example (in his recent assessment of "the American Dream") of how moral suasion and the creation of a national organization promoting a new approach to labor relations in the 1930s and 1940s led to significant change in values throughout the US business community.[108] Leonhardt observed that after the Great Depression and Franklin Roosevelt's New Deal legislative initiatives, many in the business community continued to resist new economic regulations and social policy and to fight organized labor. But following repeated election victories of Roosevelt and like-minded politicians, some business leaders began to see wisdom in accepting the New Deal's spirit of recovery, including, for example, the economic advantages of raising the wages of labor and building a productive, high-wage economy rather than focusing solely on labor cost-cutting.

Accepting this new wisdom was very much the result of missionary work of the newly formed CED, which both triggered and embodied this shift in values – starting, first, at the edges of the business community and then expanding "to shape postwar economic policy and help staff both the Truman and Eisenhower administrations."[109] The CED's purpose under the leadership of Paul Hoffman – a University of Chicago dropout who took a job at local car dealership that eventually led him to the chairmanship of Studebaker Motors – was no less than reforming the culture of American business. According to Leonhardt:

> Hoffman became an evangelist for a corporate America that was less self-interested and more concerned with the national interest. He argued that good wages were crucial to prosperity for businesses and workers alike. He figured out how to work with labor unions and government regulators, at least most of the time. He tried to persuade other executives to adopt a similar approach – and many of them did. In the 1940s and 1950s, Hoffman's vision of corporate America triumphed.[110]

All this was accomplished through moral suasion, building the case for a more collaborative or relational economic development model. Along the way, Hoffman personally recruited some of the biggest names in corporate America, "including the magazine publisher Henry Luce and top executives at Eastman Kodak, General Foods, and Lehman Brothers." Eventually, other large corporations and their CEOs joined the CED project, including Charles

---

[108] Leonhardt, *Ours Was the Shining Future,* Chapter 2.   [109] Ibid., p. 79.   [110] Ibid., p. 49.

Wilson of General Electric, who became a CED board member. Hoffman also sought advice from intellectuals such as the theologian Reinhold Niebuhr and Peter Drucker.[111] Under his leadership, the CED developed into a grassroots movement with 2,000 chapters run by local businessmen and supported by a national group providing expert advice to local chapters garnered from academic economists and Federal Reserve Bank officials. Hoffman and other CED officials toured regional gatherings of local chapters giving speeches so that local leaders could hear how their interests and work at the local level fit into an overall national effort.[112]

Committee for Economic Development's initial message was that "cost control was not the only route to profitability," and it soon expanded to include the proposition that "the twin crisis of depression and war had increased the appeal of a less rapacious version of capitalism."[113] In private, CED officials accused those remaining hard-liners outside CED as being "'intellectual Neanderthals' who believed in 'self, self, self and who were undermining the capitalist system they claimed to venerate.'"[114] By 1944, Paul Hoffman and his work with the CED was celebrated on the cover of *Time* magazine.[115] Whatever the public kudos, the basic fact was that Hoffman's campaign based on moral suasion carried to both local communities and expressed publicly at the national level converted the values of many in corporate America and probably saved the country from ideological lurches to both the left (as a result of the appeal of socialism during the 1930s) and the right (as a result to widespread fears of Communism in the 1950s).

There is a lot more to this highly organized, leader-intensive, moral suasion story, and even the barest outline of this story shows how effective moral suasion can be in the hands of committed leaders. By recruiting national opinion leaders (other CEOs) and organizing and coaching local committees of businesspeople to serve as the CED's local advocates and power sources throughout the country, Hoffman and his associates changed the course of democratic capitalism in the era before shareholder wealth maximization became a national preoccupation. Indeed, they called for and received support for an entirely new set of values and priorities in conducting business affairs: more collaboration, less self-interest.

Importantly, this moral suasion and organizing movement story is not an isolated one in recent American history. Leonhardt reports on two additional stories, both involving more distributed constellations of leadership that aimed at developing a new set of legal and economic values in the law and economics

---

[111] Ibid., p. 59.   [112] Ibid., p. 60.   [113] Ibid., p. 61 and p. 62.   [114] Ibid., p. 63.
[115] Ibid., p. 64.

professions. The first involves the creation in 1982 of a legal movement by conservative law students, supported by legal scholars, that resulted in what is now called the Federalist Society for Law and Public Policy Studies. This movement takes the form of a conservative and libertarian legal organization that advocates for a textualist and originalist interpretation of the US Constitution. The Federalist Society's statement of purpose says it was founded

> on the principles that the state exists to preserve freedom, that the separation of governmental powers is central to our Constitution, and that it is emphatically the province and duty of the judiciary to say what the law is, not what it should be. The Society seeks both to promote an awareness of these principles and to further their application through its activities.

In pursuing these activities, the Federalist Society created an extensive grassroots network of supporters and discussion participants in a Student Division with more than 10,000 students, a Lawyers Division with more than 6,500 legal professionals and others interested in the practice of law, and a Faculty Division that aims at encouraging constructive academic discourse.[116] The success of the Federal Society grassroots movement in advocating a particular legal philosophy and populating the judicial system during the Trump administration is undisputed.

The second story involves the development of the so-called neoliberal movement, which gathered force before the election of Republican Ronald Reagan as president in 1980. This emergent consensus on the right followed from years of scholarly work and public conversation that Milton Friedman initiated with several other Chicago School economists and advanced by a group of lawyers from the University of Chicago law school (including Frank Esterbrook and Antonin Scalia, who later were appointed by President Reagan, respectively, as judges on the US Court of Appeals for the 7th District and the US Supreme Court); Harvard Law School professor Douglas Ginsberg (who was appointed by President Reagan to the US Court of Appeals for the D.C. District); and Judge Robert Bork (also appointed by Reagan to the US Court of Appeals for the D.C. District after many years of scholarly work in antitrust and government regulation arena at Yale Law School). These neoliberals believed in, argued for, and disseminated opinions on limited interpretations of the US Constitution to protect individual freedoms, preserve free and open markets via deregulation of the private sector, cut taxes, restrict immigration, and a raft of social policies that, in their judgment, either violated or did not reflect the intent of the Constitution. Many of this group's neoliberal ideas and values reached a broader audience than the Reagan administration and were found to be

---

[116] https://fedsoc.org/about-us.

acceptable by many Democrats in the Clinton administration. They also lead to the deregulation of financial markets, telecoms, and airlines; the repeal of the Glass-Steagall Act of 1933; clampdowns on aggressive antitrust policy; and lowered tax rates.

These three stories about movements that shifted society's economic and political values reveal, first, that it can be done. Second, they reveal that successful efforts to socialize and build commitment to an underrepresented set of values and preferences starts with years of often scholarly homework, and then proceeds to widening circles of professional support, public education, and proselytizing through scholarly and more popular publication, speeches, and, in the case of the neoliberal movement, eventual financial support for political candidates reflecting neoliberal values.

The same progression can work to socialize the principles of fairness and reciprocity and renovate democratic capitalism. On the democracy side, scholarly work needs to continue to consolidate and package what we know about current rights to vote, rights to run for political office, the accountability of elected officials, and the impact of campaign finance and lobbying on legislating for the public interest. Fortunately, a great deal of work is underway and aimed at enhancing citizens' political participation and voice – ranging from efforts to increase voter registration and turnout to widening the field of candidates competing for political office. Much of this work has been cited in this Element.

On the capitalism side, a similar workplan needs to begin with reporting on successful collective problem-solving experiments, where reciprocal exchanges and mutual gains among economic actors have been created in a variety of negotiating and power-sharing forums around the country. My own earlier research that documented the history of the Joint Study Committee that led to creating the Saturn Corporation within General Motors Corporation is one case in point. A more recent example of such reporting is that by Rebecca Henderson on the leadership of CEO Paul Polman of Unilever in waging his campaign against palm oil production and its destructive effects on the deforestation of the rainforests. Through years of innovative collaborations with multiple stakeholders in various industry and advocacy group forums, the Sustainable Palm Oil partnership developed agreed-upon standards for cultivating sustainable palm oil. Wider-reaching forums soon followed, such as the Consumer Goods Forum, also aimed at reducing environmental contamination by consumer goods companies.[117] And this is only one story from Henderson's extensive case library. Like the creation of the Saturn Corporation, the Sustainable Palm

---

[117] Henderson, *Reimagining Capitalism in a World on Fire*, Chapter 6.

Oil partnership is the kind of field-based case study that deserves broad distribution as instructive examples of cronyism-in-reverse and successful attempts to restore environmental justice in our global political economy. There are many additional stories from the field across the nation regarding similar experiments embodying the principles of fairness and reciprocity and the delicate practice of power sharing.

As Deva Woodly, Rebecca Henderson, and others have shown, this is natural work for faculty members at business schools, schools of public policy and government, and law schools that for decades have been successful in bringing new, productive ideas to both the broad public and institutional leaders through prolific case-writing. Such scholars have researched and written about matters of management and control of complex organizations, corporate finance, international trade, defense policy, and constitutional law and precedent – just to mention a few areas where critical matters from the field have been modeled and analyzed to the benefit of practitioners.

In addition to foundational research that can motivate the socialization of a new set of governing values and reverse offending behaviors – such as pervasive cronyism and restricted suffrage – credible spokespersons and evangelists such as Paul Hoffman are required to advance the vision and build the power base needed for meaningful change. At first look, one might conclude there is a remarkable dearth of respected evangelists today. But this conclusion is not accurate. There is, in fact, an emerging cadre of intellectual leaders working on democracy renovation projects and, by direct application, the renovation of democratic capitalism as a practical governance ideal for the United States going forward. Two notable examples, already referenced, are philosophy professor and political activist Danielle Allen and law professor and political activist Lawrence Lessig, both of Harvard University. Allen founded Partners in Democracy, which works with dozens of partners in the democracy renovation space around the country focusing on voter registration, voter turnout for elections, accessibility of voting, the competitiveness of elections, ease of candidate ballot access, candidate representatives, government responsiveness, legislative and administrative transparency, and strong news coverage.[118] Lessig founded Equal Citizens, whose goal is reforming the Electoral College and Super PACs and reducing the corrosive influence of big money in politics.[119]

In addition to these established pioneers, there are many inquisitive and informed senior executives and established political leaders who could become spokespeople or evangelists, if they chose to do so – persons already working

---

[118] See https://partnersindemocracy.us.   [119] See https://equalcitizens.us.

with such organizations as the Business Roundtable, the Conference Board and its CED, the Aspen Institute, the Problem Solvers Caucus in Congress, and those serving in various state and national legislative bodies.

Never before have evangelists for a truer form of democratic capitalism had more knowledge and more grassroots and national-level democracy support groups available to them. With this intellectual and political infrastructure moving into place, the time to start socializing the norms and values comprising a supportive moral culture for democratic capitalism is at hand. Action principles have never been clearer.[120] And an implementable plan of action to renovate democratic capitalism is beginning to take shape. Others can undoubtedly add to the renovation workplan I have proposed here, but the essential elements of such a plan need to include:

- **Curbing cronyism** through reforms in campaign finance laws (including alternate campaign financing schemes that allow candidates to free themselves from large, controlling donors); federally mandated requirements for Super PACs to disclose their donors (thereby eliminating the massive presence of dark money in electoral campaigns, Congressional lobbying, and ballot initiatives); greater transparency in *corporate* reporting of campaign and lobbying spending; a slowdown in the revolving door between business and government; and, most critically, the nullification of the Supreme Court's democracy-destroying *Citizens United* decision by passing the proposed twenty-eighth amendment to the Constitution.
- **Strengthening citizen voice and influence** as a countervailing power to wealthy and influential elites (corporate and otherwise) who have captured large segments of our legislative and regulatory establishment – by improving ballot access for a more diverse population of candidates and reducing restrictions on citizens' right to vote on all candidates.
- **Working to create more democracy-supporting firms** that mirror the application of democratic principles of fairness and reciprocity in economic and political markets through selective power sharing with key constituencies and the liberation of firms from the obsessive pursuit of the problematic doctrine of shareholder wealth maximization.

---

[120] As far back as 1982, Mancor Olson in *The Rise and Decline of Nations* described how democracy suffers when special interest groups mobilize sufficient political power to steer the flow of benefits to a concentrated set of members, thereby making one of the earliest cases for curbing the influence of what we now recognize as pervasive cronyism. Similarly, in his 1992 book, *The End of History and the Last Man*, Francis Fukuyama offered a broadly compatible vision of how democracy and capitalism can combine into a better (ethically, politically, and economically) governance system. The bell has been ringing for a truly democratic capitalism for a long time.

- **Advancing a moral culture conducive to democratic capitalism** through social movement tactics that include public education and support for evangelists and spokespersons who can alert the nation to the idea that the perceived legitimacy of our system of economic and political governance can be restored by practicing the democracy principles that we teach and admire as a nation. This includes the principles of fairness, political equality, and power sharing (collaborative problem-solving) rather than individual utility maximization based on narrowly defined self-interest.

As daunting as this restoration program is, it makes little sense to wait for another existential threat or crisis to shock us into a changed mentality. Nor do we have time to wait for the moral pendulum to swing away from the currently celebrated ethos of self-serving utility maximization back in the direction of mutuality.

The longer we wait for the restoration to actuate, the more the decline of democratic capitalism as a national ideal will become irreversible. And without the restoration of our national ideal and a renewal of Americans' faith that democratic capitalism is working *for them*, rather than *against them*, social unrest and political dysfunction will inevitably accelerate.

Hopefully, Ralph Waldo Emerson's assertion – that "America is the country of tomorrow" – will be proven correct once again, with that "tomorrow" including the restoration of democratic capitalism as a credible aspiration for our country. To that end, we have great work to do together.

Appendix
The Problematic Doctrine of Shareholder Wealth Maximization

The canonization of shareholder wealth maximization as the only legitimate expression of corporate purpose over the past forty years – along with the subsequent adoption of executive compensation plans where the level of pay is tightly linked to a company's stock price – provides strong ideological and financial incentives for many US executives to disengage as a social and moral force in our political economy and focus more on how best to increase their company's stock price than on how best to contribute to a just and fair system of economic and political governance.[121]

Examples of social disengagement include persistent lack of sustained attention and investment in environmental protection; failure to ensure a rising and widely shared standard of living for hourly employees, while the compensation of senior executives continues to soar; pervasive cronyism; widespread gaming of our legislated rules-of-the-game that may benefit shareholders but offer few compensating public benefits, and lack of accountability for corporate misdeeds – just to mention a few examples.[122]

The extent of social and moral disengagement by the business and financial communities following from this narrow conception of corporate purpose makes it difficult to reverse the decline in public trust of American-style capitalism and the fraying social contract that it represents. Fortunately, we know that the purpose and governance of corporations have changed many times through the ages and that corporations can do so again when it makes good business sense to do so. Today, the incentive to recognize the limitations and costs of accepting shareholder wealth maximization as the sole, legitimate

---

[121] According to the Economic Policy Institute, vested stock awards and exercised stock options accounted for 80.1 percent of the average compensation of CEOs at the 350 largest publicly owned US firms as of 2021.

[122] In addition to social disengagement, there is a large and growing body of research that provides compelling case studies and commentary on the adverse effects of single-minded shareholder wealth maximization on the governance and competitive advantages of publicly traded firms. Recent examples include William Lazonick, "Innovation and Financialization in the Corporate Economy," Chapter 4 in Arie Y. Lewin, Greg Linden, and David J. Teece, eds., *The New Enlightenment: Reshaping Capitalism and the Global Order in the 21st Century,* Cambridge University Press, 2022; Oner Tulum, Antonio Andreoni, and William Lazonick, *From Financialization to Innovation in UK Big Pharma,* Cambridge University Press, 2022, and Charles McMillan, *The Transformation of Boeing from Technological Leadership to Financial Engineering and Decline,* Cambridge University Press, 2022.

expression of corporate purpose (and all the perverse managerial incentives that flow from such a designation) and to adopt a more inclusive definition of corporate purpose is no less than saving democratic capitalism from self-inflicted damage.

Any effort to broaden our conception of corporate purpose to include the interests of all investors and clients of a firm in matters affecting their welfare can benefit from a solid understanding of what the theoretical basis of the shareholder value maximization doctrine encompasses; how this doctrine or belief system has led to the degradation of corporate purpose and practice in recent decades; how the shareholder value maximization doctrine came to be so deeply embedded in our business culture; and what serious conceptual and practical problems are inherent in this doctrine, which have had the effect of steering corporations and their executives away from social and moral engagement with nonshareholding participants in the life of firms.

The Shareholder Wealth Maximization Doctrine

The promotion of shareholder value maximization as the only appropriate expression of corporate purpose and standard of corporate performance can be traced directly to the development and promotion of the "shareholder primacy" theory of the firm during the 1970s and 1980s. Put most simply, this theory proposes that shareholders own their corporations and that corporate managers should therefore run the corporation in their interest; in other words, managers' primary mandate is to maximize the value of the company's shares. And since shareholders are the residual bearers of risk in corporate activity – meaning that they could lose all their money without any recourse or appeal – managers have a moral obligation to protect shareholders from the "unusual degree of exposure" that they have to the corporation.[123]

While there was increasing agreement among economists and finance scholars during these years that managers ought to be focusing on enhancing the value of firms for which they worked, a question persisted about whether this was happening in practice. Were managers really working to maximize firm value? Were they truly loyal to shareholders, or were they focused on maximizing their own self-interests as predicted by various theories of managerial discretion? And, equally as important, how *should* managers behave in fulfilling their obligations to shareholders?

---

[123] Theo Vermaelen, "Maximizing Shareholder Value: An Ethical Responsibility," in Craig Smith and Gilbert Lenssen, *Mainstreaming Corporate Responsibility*, Wiley, 2009, pp. 206–218, cited in Mayer, *Prosperity*.

In 1976, Michael Jensen and William Meckling addressed these questions in a landmark paper addressing the so-called agency relationship that existed between shareholders and managers as agents of the shareholders. They also laid out a theory of the firm based on "agency theory," which, among other major contributions, made the economic case for shareholder wealth maximization as the only legitimate expression of corporate purpose and the most effective tool for minimizing the agency costs that naturally arise between principals (shareholders) and their agents (managers).[124]

The Jensen and Meckling paper reflected a rich intellectual background that extended way back in the history of economic thought to the self-interested model of humankind assumed by Bentham and also to Richard Coase's conception of the corporation as a "nexus of contracts" or series of transactions bound by "contracts" with suppliers, customers, and other parties that agree to work together for mutual benefit.[125] In the words of Jensen and Meckling:

> It is important to recognize that most organizations are *simply legal fictions which serve as a nexus for a set of contracting relationships among individuals.* ... The private corporation or firm is simply one form of a *legal fiction which serves as a nexus for contracting relationships and which is also characterized by the existence of divisible residual claims on the assets and cash flows of the organization which can generally be sold without permission of the other contracting individuals.*" (Italics are included in the original text.)[126]

What's most notable about this theory or metaphor of the firm is that it stands in sharp contrast to an alternate conception of the corporation as an entity cocreated by public authority (through state charter in the United States), which grants corporations and their managers the right to make money and operate within the constraints of certain rules of game.

According to this new theory, firms are created when internalizing contracts between owners and various factors of production into a hierarchy is efficient – that is, when the benefits of coordinating these implicit and explicit contracts and related activities in a hierarchy are greater than the costs of coordinating them through market-based transactions and when the value of the goods and services sold by the firm exceed the costs of the inputs used.

Jensen's theory posits that the efficient performance of this contractual firm requires the recognition that the primary interest of shareholders (the so-called

---

[124] Michael C. Jensen and William H. Meckling, "Theory of the Firm: Managerial Behavior, Agency Costs, and Ownership Structure," *Journal of Financial Economics*, 3, 305, 1976, pp. 305–360.

[125] Ronald H. Coase, "The Nature of the Firm," *Economica*, 4, 386, 1937, pp. 386-405.

[126] Jensen and Meckling, Theory of the Firm, p. 310.

principals) is the maximization of their wealth by professional managers (agents) – to whom significant decision rights are delegated. The theory also argues that efficient performance requires that firms adopt a system of internal governance and control that supports this primary interest.

As noted, the objective of such an internal governance and control system is minimizing whatever agency costs exist when agents (managers) behave in opportunistic ways that do not fully satisfy the interests of the principals (shareholders). These agency costs – equal to the sum of the costs of monitoring managers incurred by principals, the costs of bonding managers' interests to those of shareholders incurred by the agents, and the residual losses from agency costs that cannot be controlled – arise naturally, the argument goes, because in real organizational life managers of publicly owned firm with dispersed shareholders, who possess substantial decision and control rights over corporate resources, are rarely "perfect agents" for the owners. This is because they do not receive the full benefits of the profits earned and therefore have incentives to extract perquisites from the firm at the expense of the firm's true owners. In other words, the incentives of managers and owners are not naturally aligned.[127] Minimizing such agency costs therefore logically involves paying corporate managers in ways that tie their pay increases with share value, thereby aligning management incentives with the primary interests of shareholders – namely, the value of their investment expressed in stock price.

Agency theory immediately attracted enormous attention. Thirty years after its publication (1976), the Jensen-Meckling article was the third most cited in major economics journals.[128] The most significant management implication of this elegantly argued theory – that long-term value maximization for shareholders needs to be the primary metric for assessing the performance of business enterprise – also found a great deal of support in the financial and business communities and among faculty members in many leading business schools, including my own. Despite Michael Jensen's observation – twenty-five years after his pioneering work on agency theory appeared – that value maximization is not a vision or even a purpose and that value maximization is only a standard

---

[127] This argument echoes the conclusions of an earlier paper by Oliver Williamson, arguing that corporate managers (driven by such motives as salary, security, power, status, prestige and professional excellence) exercise their discretion over costs and resource allocation in ways that serve their personal preferences and maximize their material satisfactions – constrained only by the need to produce sufficient profits to deter interference in the operation of the firm. See Oliver E. Williamson, "Managerial Discretion and Business Behavior," *The American Economic Review*, 53, no. 5, 1963, pp. 1033–1035.

[128] J. B. Heaton, "Corporate Governance and the Cult of Agency," July 16, 2018. https://ssrn.com/abstract=3201934 or http://dx.doi.org/10.2139/ssrn.3201934. Heaton's source on citations was E. Han Kim, Adair Morse, and Luigi Zingales, "What Has Mattered to Economics Since 1970," *Journal of Economic Perspective*, 20, 2006, pp. 189, 192.

for corporate success, the performance measurement element of his management theory remains foundational to the "shareholder primacy" theory of the
firm.[129] Accordingly, the sole fiduciary duty of corporate directors and officers –
as "contractual agents" of shareholders – is to maximize shareholder wealth.[130]

How Shareholder Wealth Maximization Became So Embedded in Business Culture

Much of the appeal of this new theory of the firm and its implications for
corporate purpose was undoubtedly created by the widely read, practitioner-
oriented articles published by Michael Jensen, all of which were backed up by
more than 100 scientific papers addressing, one way or another, what he
referred to as "the struggle for organizational efficiency."[131] Along the way,
Jensen anchored his theory in a series of conceptual building blocks and a series
of published case studies, which provided him with the platform he needed to
address what he saw as capitalism's principal shortcomings – uncontrolled
agency costs and unresponsive corporate governance practices – and a variety
of proposals for reversing what he saw as the breakdown in the internal control
systems of large firms. In addition to his writings, Jensen's public lectures and
oversubscribed classes at the Harvard Business School, from which generations
of students launched careers in investment banking, private equity, management consulting, and corporate management, brought him great popularity and,
in some quarters, notoriety. For all these reasons, Jensen became one of the best-
known and influential business economists spanning the Millennium, even as
his work was being challenged by academic colleagues and students who had
entirely different conceptions of what role corporations served, and needed to
serve, in contemporary society. To many audiences, however, Jensen's ideas
about the coordination, control, and management of organizations "made
sense." And, in many respects, they did.

For example, many of Jensen's students and fans in industry were just as
concerned as he was about failure of the internal control systems of large, public
firms, which was the subject of his 1993 presidential address to the American
Finance Association.[132] After analyzing the performance of large public firms

---

[129] Michael C. Jensen, "Value Maximization, Stakeholder Theory, and the Corporate Objective
Function," *Business Ethics Quarterly*,12, no. 2, January 2002, pp. 235–256.

[130] Jensen and Meckling, Theory of the Firm, pp. 305, 311.

[131] Some of the most widely read and influential articles were published in the *Harvard Business
Review*: Michael C. Jensen, "Eclipse of the Public Corporation," *Harvard Business Review*
(September–October 1989); Michael C. Jensen, and Kevin J. Murphy. "CEO Incentives: It's
Not How Much You Pay, but How," *Harvard Business Review*, 68, no. 3 (May–June 1990); and
Michael C. Jensen, "Corporate Budgeting Is Broken, Let's Fix It," *Harvard Business Review*,
79, no. 10, November 2001.

during the 1980–90 in preparation for this address and its accompanying paper, Jensen reported that a large proportion were unable to earn their cost of capital (due to major inefficiencies in in their capital expenditures and R&D spending) on a sustained basis. From these findings of low investment returns and the widespread destruction of economic value in large firms (particularly those without monopoly power) during the 1980s, it seemed straightforward that Jensen's advocacy for aggressive pursuit of shareholder value maximization, coupled with compatible governance reforms, was the proper antidote for the number of underperformers. Many in academia and the business community agreed.

In addition, Jensen's concerns about underperforming firms coincided with the development of the market for corporate control which blossomed in the 1980s, and his arguments in favor of hostile takeovers as a disciplining device for inefficient firms immediately found support from buy-out firms, who's widely debated and oft-criticized takeover strategies suddenly found an elegant, academic validation. Starting in the 1980s, almost a quarter of public firms in the United States were the target of attempted hostile takeovers opposed by a firm's management and another quarter received takeover bids supported by management.[133] In this environment, Michael Jensen's carefully argued rationale for shareholder value maximization and equity-based pay (as a way of reducing agency costs) was quickly picked up and embraced by buyout firms and takeover specialists seeking economic justification for supposedly value creating strategies (one-third of which eventually turned out not to be, due to insolvencies stemming from an excess use of debt to finance takeovers[134]).

Another source of popularity of this new theory of the firm and expression of corporate purpose was that it offered corporate executives and financial analysts a simple, theoretically justifiable performance measure (stock price) that captured the present value of all future effects – namely, firm value. As Jensen famously wrote in 2002:

> Any organization must have a single-valued objective as a precursor to purposeful or rational behavior. ... It is logically impossible to maximize in more than one dimension at the same time. ... Thus, telling a manager to maximize current profits, market share, future growth profits, and anything else one pleases will leave that manager with no way to make a reasoned decision. In effect, it leaves the manager with no objective.[135]

---

[132] Michael C. Jensen, "The Modern Industrial Revolution, Exit, and the Failure of Internal Control Systems," *The Journal of Finance*, 48, no. 3, July 1993, pp. 831–880.

[133] Mark Mitchell and J. Harold Mulherin, "The Impact of Industry Shocks on Takeover and Restructuring Activity, *Journal of Financial Economics*, 41, no. 2, June 1996, pp. 193–229.

[134] Bengt Holmstrom and Steven N. Kaplan, "Corporate Governance and Merger Activity in the U.S.: Making Sense of the 1980s and 1990s," NBER Working Paper No. 8220, April 2001.

From here, it was an easy step to place firm value at the center of corporate conscience.

Finally, the contractual theory of the firm, buttressed by agency theory, seemed to validate the argument of soon-to-be Nobel Lauriat Milton Friedman, whose voice in his famous 1970 *New York Times* article rang loud and clear throughout the business community and continues to resonate today in many classrooms and boardrooms.[136] Friedman argued that a manager's primary duty is to maximize the value of shareholders' capital because it maximizes the chance of capitalism to allocate capital freely in the service of individual needs, promotes economic efficiency, preserves individual freedoms, and maintains the trust that shareholders place in managers to serve their interests. At base, this was a normative, ethical argument. In this way, the concept of shareholder value maximization was co-branded by two of the leading lights of the Chicago school of economics (where Freidman was a professor and Jensen received his doctorate.)

Conceptual and Practical Problems with This Revisionist Theory of Corporate Purpose

Criticisms of this revisionist conception of the firm and corporate purpose have persisted for many reasons. Three deserve special comment here.

To start, the well-functioning of market economies and firms requires more than shareholder value maximization as a motivating principle.[137] To operate functionally, firms need to work hard at building and retaining the mutual trust and confidence of constituencies beyond shareholders. Entrepreneurship, which involves the assembly of complementary resources and skills, cannot be practiced in the absence of cooperation and mutual trust among enterprise members. And apart from entrepreneurial startups, shareholders are rarely the sole group that provide specialized inputs to corporate production and make essential contributions to an enterprise's success.[138] Executives, rank-and-file employees, creditors, and even members of a local community also make essential contributions. For all these reasons, in the absence of cooperation and mutual trust, the costs of coordination and commitment will skyrocket, and the social legitimacy of market-based institutions will be under relentless challenge.

---

[135] Jensen, "Value Maximization, Stakeholder Theory, and the Corporate Objective Function."

[136] Milton Friedman, "The Social Responsibility of Business Is to Increase Profits."

[137] See, for example, R. Edward Freeman, Kirtsen E. Martin., and Bidhan L, Parmar, "Stakeholder Capitalism," *Journal of Business Ethics*, 74, no. 4, 2007, pp. 303–314.

[138] Margaret M. Blair and Lynn A. Stout, "A Team Production Theory of Corporate Law," *Virginia Law Review*, 85, no. 2, March 1999, pp. 247–328.

Second, the striking metaphor of the firm as a "nexus of contracts" with attendant principal-agent problems that only a focus on shareholder value maximization can mitigate is also too simple an analogy. Corporations, in their everyday operation, are far more than a "nexus of contracts" through which business transactions are carried out – although associating with a corporate entity through contracts and law to pursue self-interest is certainly part of the creation story. But contracts do not exhaust the reciprocal understanding on which the productivity of firms rests. Supracontractual understandings or voluntary reciprocal exchanges with stakeholders are also required for corporations to be successful.[139] For example, relationships with "internal stakeholders" (directors, executives, employees, and their unions) comprise the teamwork necessary for production and the mutual benefits flowing from that production. However, in this production team the contributions of each manager and worker are difficult to observe and ascribe to specific bits of production. Since it is impossible to contractually specify all the ways team members need to cooperate for efficient production, and since excessive monitoring is likely to depress morale and breed "reciprocal distrust," well-managed firms develop norms or trust and reciprocity among members in return for contractually unguaranteed rewards such as bonuses, promotions, better working conditions, family leaves, and so forth. For similar reasons, relationships with "external stakeholders" (suppliers, customers, and communities in which the corporation does business) require similarly reciprocal normative understandings beyond contractual guarantees.

On this basis alone, it does not make much sense to view the firm simply as a nexus of contracts. Rather, it makes more sense to view the firm, in Elizabeth Anderson's words, as

> a joint enterprise constituted by a nexus of cooperative relationships in which internal stakeholders commit firm-specific assets to relatively long-term team production arrangements, submit to common governance, and repeatedly interact on the basis of norms of trust and reciprocity, all for mutual and reciprocal benefit, the terms of which are not exhausted by law and contract. The firm also typically enters into protracted reciprocal relationships with external stakeholders ... which are supported by normative expectations of trust, reciprocity, and mutual gain, not all of which are defined in explicit contracts.[140]

---

[139] Elizabeth Anderson, "The Business Enterprise as an Ethical Agent," in Subramanian Rangan, ed., *Performance and Progress: Essays on Capitalism, Business, and Society*, Oxford University Press, 2015, pp. 185–202.

[140] Ibid., p. 91 and pp. 189–90.

The most important implication of this conception of the firm is that directors owe a fiduciary duty to the corporation itself, not to the shareholders exclusively, and shareholder value maximization as a singular definition of corporate purpose under market capitalism is inappropriate.

Finally, the new theory of the firm is detached from evolving ideas about the legal status of shareholder claims on the public corporation. It is axiomatic in the world of capitalism that those who have placed risk capital into an enterprise through their shareholdings deserve a satisfactory return on that capital (the minimum return determined by the riskiness of the investment). It is less axiomatic, but nevertheless supported by an array of legal scholars, organization theorists, business leaders, and members of the investment community that the interests of other constituencies comprising the firm need to be justly served as well (whatever justly means in case-specific situations) to ensure corporate stability and perpetuity.[141]

Over the years, a variety of legal opinions and legislation have supported this view of corporate purpose. Today, US corporate law does not impose upon management an exclusive profit-maximizing duty, but merely links directors' and managers' fiduciary responsibilities to the corporation's and stockholders' long-term interests. While Delaware's corporate statute (directly relevant to the 60 percent of publicly traded corporations that are incorporated in the state of Delaware) is not totally precise on the matter of corporate purpose, the state's case law does convey a precise opinion on the matter. For example, after the court affirmed in the Revlon case that corporate directors must put the interests of shareholders first in the case of takeovers and competitive takeovers bids (by accepting the highest price offered once they decided to put the company up for sale), it clearly left the door open for a more pluralistic conception of corporate purpose if doing so serves the interests of nonshareholders in a way that is rationally related to shareholder interests.[142] This accommodation of plural interests is perfectly consistent with subsequent court opinions validating non-maximizing shareholder value in the short term in order to achieve corporate success in the long run, such as in the Eastman Chemical Co. case.[143] Indeed,

---

[141] See, for example, Margaret M. Blair and Lynn A. Stout, "A Team Production Theory of Corporate Law." Stout, *The Shareholder Value Myth*, Berrett-Koehler, 2012; Chester I Barnard, *The Function of the Executive*, Harvard University Press, 1950; and R. Edward Freeman, *Strategic Management: A Stakeholder Approach*, Pitman Publishing, Inc., 1984, and Lynn Paine, *Value Shift: Why Companies Must Merge Social and Financial Imperatives to Achieve Superior Performance*, McGraw-Hill, 2003.

[142] Revlon, Inc. v. MacAndrews & Forbes Holdings, Inc., 506 A.2d 173 (Del. (1985). See also eBay Domestic Holdings, Inc. v. Newmark, 16 A.3d 1 (Del. Ch. 2010).

[143] 18 Virtus Capital L.P. v. Eastman Chem. Co., Civ. A. No. 9808-VCL, 2015 WL 580553, at *16 n.5 (Del. Ch. Feb. 11, 2015).

what Delaware case law has revealed is a definite preference for corporations focusing on longevity rather than current shareholder value maximization.

It is clear that members of the Supreme Court are largely in agreement with the Delaware court. As Justice Samuel Alito noted in *Burwell* v. *Hobby Lobby Stores, Inc.* (2014), "While it is certainly true that a central objective of for-profit corporations is to make money, modern corporate law does not require for-profit corporations to pursue profit at the expense of everything else, and many do not do so."

A statement issued in August 2019 by the Business Roundtable, comprised of the nation's most powerful CEOs, goes a step further. The Roundtable statement, signed by 181 CEOs, reversed its long-held position on shareholder wealth maximization as the most appropriate expression of corporate purpose. Signatories acknowledged that adopting a more balanced vision of corporate purpose serving all stakeholder needs – by investing in employees, delivering value to customers, dealing ethically with suppliers, and supporting outside communities – "is the only way to be successful over the long run." The statement declares that serving these needs is now at the forefront of American business goals. For this claim to prove true, reciprocity and powersharing will need to become more prominent governance norms.

Bibliography

Allen, Danielle, *Talking to Strangers: Anxieties of Citizenship since Brown v. Board of Education*, University of Chicago Press, 2004.

Allen, Danielle, *Justice by Means of Democracy*, The University of Chicago Press, 2023.

Anderson, Elizabeth, "The Business Enterprise as an Ethical Agent," in Subramanian Rangan, ed., *Performance and Progress: Essays on Capitalism, Business, and Society*, Oxford University Press, pp. 185–202, 2015.

Anderson, Elizabeth, *Private Government*, Princeton University Press, 2017.

Bahat, Roy E., Kochan, Thomas A., and Rubensteain, Liba W., "The Labor Savvy Leader," *Harvard Business Review*, July–August 2023.

Bebchuk, Lucian A., Jackson, Robert J., Jr., Nelson, James D., and Tallarita, Roberto, "The Untenable Case for Keeping Investors in the Dark," *Harvard Business Law Review*, Vol. 10, 2019.

Blair, Margaret M. and Stout, Lynn A., "A Team Production Theory of Corporate Law," *Virginia Law Review*, 85, no. 2, 247–328, March 1999.

Bower, Joseph L., Leonard, Herman B., and Paine, Lynn S., *Capitalism at Risk*, Harvard Business Review Press, 2011.

Clements, Jeffrey D., "But It Will Happen": A Constitutional Amendment to Secure Political Equality in Election Spending and Representation, *Harvard Law & Policy Review*, 13, 373–419, 2019.

Coase, Ronald H., "The Nature of the Firm," *Economica*, 4, 386, 386–405, 1937.

Collier, Paul, *The Future of Capitalism*, HarperCollins, 2018.

Downs, Anthony, *An Economic Theory of Democracy*, Harper, 1957.

Dyer, Davis, Salter, Malcolm S., and Webber, Alan M., *Changing Alliances*, Harvard Business School Press, 1987.

Freeman, R. Edward, Martin, Kirtsen E., and Parmar, Bidhan L., "Stakeholder Capitalism," *Journal of Business Ethics*, 74, no. 4, 303–314, 2007.

Friedman, Milton, "The Social Responsibility of Business Is to Increase Profits," *New York Times Magazine*, September 13, 1970.

Fukuyama, Francis, *The End of History and the Last Man*, Free Press, 1992.

Gilens, Martin and Page, Benjamin I., "Testing Theories of American Politics: Elites, Interest Groups, and Average Citizens," *Perspectives on Politics*, American Political Science Association, 12, no. 3, 564–581, September 2014.

Granovetter, Mark, "The Social Construction of Corruption," in Victor Nee and Richard Swerdling, eds., *On Capitalism*, Stanford University Press, pp. 152–172, 2007.

Hanauer, Nick and Beinhocker, Eric, "Capitalism Redefined," *Democracy: A Journal of Ideas*, no. 31, Winter 2014, https://democracyjournal.org/magazine/31/capitalism-redefined/.

Henderson, Rebecca, "The Business Case for Saving Democracy," *Harvard Business Review*, March 10, 2020.

Henderson, Rebecca, *Reimaging Capitalism in a World on Fire*, Public Affairs, 2020.

Iversen, Torben and Soskice, David, *Democracy and Prosperity*, Princeton University Press, 2019.

Jensen, Michael C., "Eclipse of the Public Corporation," *Harvard Business Review*, September–October 1989.

Jensen, Michael C., "The Modern Industrial Revolution, Exit, and the Failure of Internal Control Systems," *The Journal of Finance*, 48, no. 3, 831–880, July 1993.

Jensen, Michael C., "Self-Interest, Altruism, Incentives, and Agency Theory," *Journal of Applied Corporate Finance*, 7, no. 2, 40–45, Summer 1994.

Jensen, Michael C., *Foundations of Organizational Strategy*, Harvard University Press, 1998.

Jensen, Michael C., *A Theory of the Firm: Governance, Residual Claims, and Organizational Forms*, Harvard University Press, 2000.

Jensen, Michael C., "Corporate Budgeting Is Broken, Let's Fix It," *Harvard Business Review*, 79, no. 10, November 2001.

Jensen, Michael C., "Value Maximization, Stakeholder Theory, and the Corporate Objective Function," *Business Ethics Quarterly*, 12, no. 2, 235–256, January 2002.

Jensen, Michael C. and Meckling, William H., "Theory of the Firm: Managerial Behavior, Agency Costs, and Ownership Structure," *Journal of Financial Economics*, 3, 305–360, 1976.

Jensen, Michael C. and Murphy, Kevin J.. "CEO Incentives: It's Not How Much You Pay, but How," *Harvard Business Review*, 68, no. 3, May–June 1990.

Jones, Geoffrey, *Deeply Responsible Business: A Global History of Value-Driven Leadership*, Harvard University Press, 2023.

Kaiser, Robert G., *So Damn Much Money: The Triumph of Lobbying and the Corrosion of American Government*, Vintage Books, 2010.

Kaiser, Robert G., *Act of Congress: How America's Essential Institution Works, and How It Doesn't*, Knopf, 2013.

Lapore, Jill, "The United States' Unamendable Constitution," *The New Yorker*, October 26, 2022.

Lazonick, William, "Innovation and Financialization in the Corporate Economy," Chapter 4 in Arie Y. Lewin, Greg Linden, and David J. Teece, eds., *The New Enlightenment: Reshaping Capitalism and the Global Oder in the 21st Century*, Cambridge University Press, 2022.

Leonhardt, David, *Ours Was the Shining Future*, Random House, 2023.

Lessig, Lawrence, *Republic, Lost: How Money Corrupts Congress – and a Plan to Stop It*, Hachette Book Group, 2015.

Lewis, Hunter, *Crony Capitalism in America: 2008–2012*, AC^2 Books, 2013.

Mayer, Colin, *Firm Commitment*, Oxford University Press, 2013.

Mayer, Colin, *Prosperity*, Oxford University Press, 2018.

McCraw, Thomas K., *Creating Modern Capitalism*, Harvard University Press, 1998.

McMillan, Charles, *The Transformation of Boeing from Technological Leadership to Financial Engineering and Decline*, Cambridge University Press, 2022.

Mokyr, Joel, *A Culture of Growth: The Origins of the Modern Economy*, Princeton University Press, 2016.

Novak, Michael, *The Spirit of Democratic Capitalism*, Simon & Schuster, 1982.

Novak, Michael, "Democratic Capitalism," *National Review*, September 24, 2013.

Olson, Mancor, *The Rise and Decline of Nations*, Yale University Press, 1982.

Paine, Lynn, *Value Shift: Why Companies Must Merge Social and Financial Imperatives to Achieve Superior Performance*, McGraw-Hill, 2003.

Rajan, Raghuram and Zingales, Luigi, *Saving Capitalism from the Capitalists*, Princeton University Press, 2004.

Rawls, John, *Justice as Fairness*, Harvard University Press, 2001.

Reich, Robert B., *Saving Capitalism: For the Many, Not the Few*, Knopf, 2015.

Ross, Stephen A., "The Economic Theory of Agency," *The American Economic Review*, 63, 134–139, 1973.

Salter, Malcolm S., "Crony Capitalism, American Style: What Are We Talking about Here?" October 22, 2014. Harvard Business School Research Paper Series No. 15–025. https://ssrn.com/abstract=2513490.

Salter, Malcolm S., "Sugar-Coated Capitalism Is No Free Market," *Forbes*, November 16, 2015. www.forbes.com/sites/realspin/2015/11/16/sugar-coated-capitalism-is-no-free-market/.

Scott, Bruce R., *Capitalism: Its Origins and Evolution as a System of Governance*, Springer, 2011.

Slobodian, Quinn, *Globalists*, Harvard University Press, 2018.

Smith, Herrick, *Who Stole the American Dream?* Random House, 2012.

Soudek, Josef, "Aristotle's Theory of Exchange: An Inquiry into the Origin of Economic Analysis," *Proceedings of the American Philosophical Society*, 96, no. 1, 45–75, February 1952.

Stiglitz, Joself E., *The Price of Inequality*, W.W. Norton, 2013.

Stockman, David A., *The Great Deformation: The Corruption of Capitalism in America*, Public Affairs, 2013.

Stout, Lynn, *The Shareholder Value Myth*, Berrett-Koehler, 2012.

Streek, Wolfgang, "The Crises of Democratic Capitalism," *New Left Review*, September/October 2011.

Streek, Wolfgang, "How Will Capitalism End?" *New Left Review*, May/June 2014.

Strine, Leo E. and Walter, Nicholas, "Originalist or Original: The Difficulties of Reconciling *Citizens United* with Corporate Law History," The Harvard John M. Olin Discussion Paper No. 81, February 13, 2015.

Swindler, Ann, "Culture in Action: Symbols and Strategies," *American Sociological Review*, 51, no. 2, 273–286, April 1986.

Teece, David J., *The New Enlightenment: Reshaping Capitalism and the Global Oder in the 21st Century*, Cambridge University Press, 2022.

Tulum, Oner, Andreoni, Antonio, and Lazonick, William, *From Financialization to Innovation in UK Big Pharma*, Cambridge University Press, 2022.

Upham, David, "The Primacy of Property Rights and the American Founding," *Foundation of Economic Education*, February 1, 1998.

Vermaelen, Theo, "Maximizing Shareholder Value: An Ethical Responsibility," in Craig Smith and Gilbert Lenssen, eds., *Mainstreaming Corporate Responsibility*, Wiley, pp. 206–218, 2009.

Will, George, "The Limits of Majority Rule," *National Affairs*, Summer 2001.

Williamson, Oliver E., "Managerial Discretion and Business Behavior," *The American Economic Review*, 53, no. 5, 1032–1057, 1963.

Wolf, Martin, *The Crisis of Democratic Capitalism*, Penguin Press, 2023.

Woodly, Deva R., *Reckoning: Black Lives Matter and the Democratic Necessity of Social Movements*, Oxford University Press, 2022.

Zingales, Luigi, *A Capitalism for the People*, Basic Books, 2012.

Zitner, Aaron, "Voters See American Dream Slipping Out of Reach," *The Wall Street Journal*, November 24, 2023.

Cambridge Elements ☰

Reinventing Capitalism

Arie Y. Lewin
Duke University

Arie Y. Lewin is Professor Emeritus of Strategy and International Business at Duke University, Fuqua School of Business. He is an Elected Fellow of the Academy of International Business and a Recipient of the Academy of Management inaugural Joanne Martin Trailblazer Award. Previously, he was Editor-in-Chief of *Management and Organization Review* (2015–2021) and the *Journal of International Business Studies* (2000–2007), founding Editor-in-Chief of Organization Science (1989–2007), and Convener of Organization Science Winter Conference (1990–2012). His research centers on studies of organizations' adaptation as co-evolutionary systems, the emergence of new organizational forms, and adaptive capabilities of innovating and imitating organizations. His current research focuses on de-globalization and decoupling, the Fourth Industrial Revolution, and the renewal of capitalism.

Till Talaulicar
University of Erfurt

Till Talaulicar holds the Chair of Organization and Management at the University of Erfurt where he is also the Dean of the Faculty of Economics, Law and Social Sciences. His main research expertise is in the areas of corporate governance and the responsibilities of the corporate sector in modern societies. Professor Talaulicar is Editor-in-Chief of *Corporate Governance: An International Review*, Senior Editor of Management and Organization Review and serves on the Editorial Board of Organization Science. Moreover, he has been Founding Member and Chairperson of the Board of the International Corporate Governance Society (2014–2020).

About the Series

This series seeks to feature explorations about the crisis of legitimacy facing capitalism today, including the increasing income and wealth gap, the decline of the middle class, threats to employment due to globalization and digitalization, undermined trust in institutions, discrimination against minorities, global poverty and pollution. Being grounded in a business and management perspective, the series incorporates contributions from multiple disciplines on the causes of the current crisis and potential solutions to renew capitalism.

Panmure House is the final and only remaining home of Adam Smith, Scottish philosopher and 'Father of modern economics.' Smith occupied the House between 1778 and 1790, during which time he completed the final editions of his master works: The Theory of Moral Sentiments and The Wealth of Nations. Other great luminaries and thinkers of the Scottish Enlightenment visited Smith regularly at the House across this period. Their mission is to provide a world-class twenty-first-century centre for social and economic debate and research, convening in the name of Adam Smith to effect positive change and forge global, future-focussed networks.

ADAM SMITH
PANMURE
HOUSE

Cambridge Elements ≡

Reinventing Capitalism

Printed in the United States
by Baker & Taylor Publisher Services